Who Are My Brothers?

Who Are My
Brothers?

Philip Armstrong, CSC, Editor

ALBA·HOUSE NEW·YORK

SOCIETY OF ST. PAUL, 2187 VICTORY BLVD., STATEN ISLAND, NEW YORK 10314

Library of Congress Cataloging-in-Publication Data

Who are my brothers?
    Includes bibliographies.
    1. Monasticism and religious orders.   2. Lay
brothers.   3. Brothers (in religious orders,
congregations, etc.)   4. Catholic Church — Clergy.
I.   Armstrong, Philip, C.S.C.
BX2432.W47   1988   255'.092   88-6351
ISBN 0-8189-0533-6

Designed, printed and bound in the United States of
America by the Fathers and Brothers of the
Society of St. Paul, 2187 Victory Boulevard,
Staten Island, New York 10314, as part of their
communications apostolate.

Printing Information:

Current Printing - first digit   1   2   3   4   5   6   7   8   9   10   11   12   13   14   15   16   17   18   19   20

Year of Current Printing - first year shown

    1988   1989   1990   1991   1992   1993   1994   1995   1996   1997   1998   1999   2000   2001   2002

A study of the relationships experienced between clerical and lay religious in men's congregations in the United States of America, sponsored by the Conference of Major Superiors of Men.

Foreword

REV. STEPHEN TUTAS, S.M.
President

S EVERAL YEARS AGO CMSM published a paper on "Clericalism." This essay was used extensively within religious communities and beyond. CMSM then set up a task force to further this study, focusing on "the relationship between lay and priest religious in communities of men religious."

This book articulates and shares one dimension of our experience of religious life as men religious. The theme of the relationship of brothers and priests is most appropriate for our time as it helps to underline the identity of religious life independently of the ordained ministry — in fact, of any ministry. It highlights the unifying value of fraternity in a religious community. I believe this emphasis on community is especially meaningful for the Church in our time. It is my hope that religious communities can help to show the fundamental unifying value of baptismal consecration and also help to encourage us in our efforts to build up the Church in our day, a Church that engages every member and recognizes the complementarity of the varied gifts with which we as Church are blessed.

I consider it a great privilege to be able to present this volume for your prayerful reflection. I am most encouraged when the

Conference of Major Superiors of Men Religious is able to facilitate the sharing of hopes and concerns among religious and also stimulate discussion of religious issues with other groups in the Church. In the final analysis, this book is about relationships in a community of faith.

Table of Contents

II. Experiential Reflections On Cleric-Lay
Relationships

III. Analysis Of Responses

Introduction

REV. ROLAND J. FALEY, T.O.R.
Executive Director, CMSM

T HIS STUDY IS not intended to be partisan, even though the tone of some articles may seem to be so. It is conceived as a priest-brother study, not a brother versus priest problem. Its urgency flows from the call of the Second Vatican Council for a deeper and better understanding of what it means to be a religious.

Reasons are multiple why priesthood has so overshadowed brotherhood. Many of them are discussed in these pages. On the one hand, there is little doubt that men who chose to be brothers did so for a clearly defined purpose — they wanted to be religious. They saw their vocation in these terms and there the case rested. As for those who chose priesthood in a religious institute, the picture was not that clear. Religious life was certainly part of the choice but not always the dominant factor. For many people, had the possibility of priesthood been excluded, the religious state would not have been chosen. Frequently it seemed that the major moments of religious life (e.g. novitiate and profession) were geared ultimately toward ordination. It was clear that priest and brother moved on different tracks.

Much of this has changed dramatically and for a variety of reasons.

Theologically, religious life has emerged more clearly as a distinct calling, quite apart from other ministries to which it may be related. Without any concerted effort to de-emphasize priesthood, there is now a greater stress on the commonality of the religious state and its independent value. At the same time, there has been stronger emphasis on the priesthood not in terms of status but as a ministry of service.

Culturally we live in a time in which preferential status, when granted and not earned, receives scant acceptance. Privilege does not sit well with present day society, even less when it revolves around Church positions. This equalizing tendency has brought with it the desire to extend offices and opportunities to all religious in an institute. In the American culture brothers and priests receive an identical or, at least, equivalent formative preparation for ministry. The ardent hope that all canonical offices will be open to all religious within religious institutes, as long as it is in keeping with the original charism, has reached the attention and consideration of the Church's major authorities. The last few decades have witnessed remarkable progress.

Religious communities made up exclusively of brothers have not escaped the shadows of subordination. While respected as educators, social service experts and the like, they have been all too often seen through the prism of a priestly vocation, one to which they feel no personal inclination or calling. The oft-repeated question directed to brothers: "Why didn't you go all the way?" shows a level of perception (or lack thereof) of the real meaning of the religious life.

The present work attempts to evaluate this reality. It is meant to be positive and constructive, while not sacrificing frankness and candor. It reflects the conviction that religious life is an indispensable gift of gospel witness in the Church's life, just as priesthood is a gift which ensures the continued presence of Eucharistic and sacramental life.

The book looks at the question from a variety of viewpoints. The principal article gives an overview of the historical dimension of the priest-brother relationship. Subsequent chapters look at the cultural, theological, psychological and canonical aspects. Personal experience is reflected in those articles by a layman and men and women religious describing their perception of the priest-brother reality.

This book will be of particular interest to men religious in this country and elsewhere since they are directly affected by the issue. But since the brother-priest question deals with a theological and cultural issue with broad ramifications, it will shed light on other ecclesial realities wherein both unity and tension are present. Men and women religious as well as the laity should find the study timely and interesting.

The book follows a sequence which may need explanation. For obvious reasons the historical chapter is inaugural and pivotal since it brings us to the point where we currently stand. History is experienced in a given culture, in a theological milieu, and in a determined sociological setting. The first part of the book concludes with the way in which the relationship of priests and brothers has been codified in law. It establishes a fixed point indicating how far we have come and opens up potential development for the future.

The second part is entirely experiential in character reflecting on the manner in which the priest-brother relationship is lived by some and perceived by others. The epilogue is both an end and a beginning in terms of future direction. The results of the U.S. survey of attitudes and beliefs are found in part three.

The Conference of Major Superiors of Men (CMSM) undertook this study to assist leadership in religious life and the Church at large in their assessment of the profound evolution taking place in this area, as well as to offer to all interested readers the chance to sharpen their perspective. Above all, it is presented in the service of religious life.

A companion study to this present volume deals with the prevailing attitudes of religious today on this question. A random sampling of some three thousand American religious was sent an extensive questionnaire. The results have been tabulated and analyzed to serve as an important index to the extent to which we are dealing with a common concern. A summary of the study appears in the third part of this book.

The Conference is indebted to the task force which planned the present volume and assigned and edited the articles: Philip Armstrong, C.S.C., editor, Jordan Hite, T.O.R., and in a special way, Justin Der, O.F.M. Cap., whose untimely death at an early age made this project his last on this earth. David Nygren, C.M., is the valued designer and executor of the attitudinal study. The Lilly Foundation of Indianapolis funded the entire study and merits our gratitude for this and much more.

It is often said that the vocation to religious life emerges with the greatest clarity in the life of the brother, when his role is properly understood. The priesthood is a salutary complement to this calling when seen as an added dimension of service in ministry. As the present study shows, the balance between the two has not always been harmoniously maintained. But in learning from the mistakes of the past, we will hopefully be less inclined to repeat them. In this way, both brothers and priests are certain to gain as they witness to the perennial values of religious life.

I. Reflections on Cleric-Lay Relationships in Men's Religious Communities

Historical Development of Brother-Priest Relationships

REV. JAMES FITZ, S.M.

Introduction

T HE RELATIONSHIP between religious life and ordained ministry is being seriously rethought in our post-Vatican II Church. It is clear that the two are separate but compatible charisms in the Church. Religious life is not essential to ordained ministry; ordained ministry is not essential to religious life. Religious life as described by Vatican Council II is "a form of life to which some Christians, both clerical and lay, are called by God so that they may enjoy a special gift of grace in the life of the Church and may contribute, each in their own way, to the mission of the Church." [1] The ordained ministry (bishop, presbyter, deacon) relates to the order (hierarchy) of the Church. The religious life relates to the witness (lifestyle) of the Church. The graces of ordained ministry and religious life can both be active in the life of a person. But they are separate gifts of the Holy Spirit.

As we study any phenomenon in the Church, we find an historical perspective to be an essential element. History frees us from the illusion that present practice is the one and only traditional

3

practice. A study of history in this chapter will help us to understand the rich tradition of the charism of religious life within the
Church, especially the relationship of clerics and non-clerics in
men's religious institutes. Religious life has changed as it has
responded to different times and different cultures. It is open to
change in the future to the degree that religious are freed from being
locked into one culture and time perspective. It is hoped that this
brief historical overview will help us appreciate this one aspect of
the history of religious life and use its traditions creatively as we
move into the future. Ideally we will be rooted in the "Tradition"
without being stuck in any particular "tradition."

There are several preliminary remarks that will help us in the
study of the history of the relationship between clerics and non-
clerics in men's religious institutes.

First, the charism of religious life has been manifested in
various ways in the history of the Church. The definition of
religious life by the Church is different today from what it was in
earlier eras. For example, members of religious institutes having
simple vows were not considered religious by the Church until the
early 20th century. In this chapter, then, we will reflect on the
history of those groups that have chosen to live their "life as
parable"[2] or as "active prophecy."[3]. These groups are
communities that have an ordered life and a public commitment to
the values inherent in the traditional "evangelical counsels" of
poverty, chastity, and obedience.[4]

Second, our day calls for a new examination of the history.
Since history is always interpreted in light of present events, new
events and new experiences in the Church in our day have led us to
reflect anew on our history. The richness and diversity of that
history is a treasure to be mined. Each new challenge in our
pilgrimage back to God offers us an opportunity to re-examine our
tradition for the treasures that may be helpful for the moment.
"Every scribe who is learned in the reign of God is like the head of

a household who can bring from the storeroom both the new and the old'' (Matthew 13:52).

Third, any good historian knows that the search for ''objective'' history is an impossible quest. The word ''historical'' appears in the title of this chapter. Although every attempt has been made to write this history on as broad a foundation of factual data as possible, the very facts chosen and their interpretation are inevitably subjective. This chapter is also affected by the limitations of any overview of history. Obviously the field for this study is vast and this study will need to make some generalizations. It is important to remember that at any time in history there are usually several currents of thought on any issue. Even within any one religious order at any given period, there is rarely unanimity of thought.

Finally, the history of the relationship between clerics and non-clerics in male religious communities often reflects the relationship between clerics and lay people in the whole Church at any particular point in history. The stratification of cultures into classes and the attitudes of these classes toward one another has also affected attitudes in religious communities. These relationships are an important background motif for our study.

The hope of this chapter is, then, to give an overview of the relationship of clerics and non-clerics in men's religious institutes throughout history in order to give a context to our present-day discussion. In the context of the limitations discussed above, I do believe that the major relationships are exposed and a solid foundation given for reflection on our reality today.

There are many ways to divide the eras of the history of religious life. In this study we will follow, with some modification, the eras described in the article, ''The Recovery of Religious Life'' by Larry Cada, S.M. and Raymond Fitz, S.M.[5] After some preliminary reflections on the early Church, we will try to describe the relationship between clerics and non-clerics in the major eras of religious life history:

The Desert Tradition (250-500)
Monasticism (500-1200)
    The rise of the monastic movement
    The renewal of the monastic movement
Mendicant Orders (1200-1500)
Apostolic Orders (1500-1800)
Age of Institutional Ministries (1800-present)

The Desert Tradition

ALTHOUGH THE ORIGIN of religious life, per se, is normally dated from the middle of the third century, there were antecedents of religious life that shaped the atmosphere in which it developed. There were three lifestyles (forms of witness) that contributed to the milieu in which religious life arose:

1.   *Prophecy* — when the charismatic itinerant prophets of the early Church disappeared, a void was created that religious life filled.

2.   *Widows and virgins* — These women (and some men) provided a model of life that included celibate chastity, asceticism, prayer and good works, a model that was taken up by religious.

3.   *Martyrs* — The martyrs' radical following of Christ made them the early Church heroes. With the end of the age of persecutions, the radical following of Christ developed new forms and the Church needed new heroes. Early religious life was influenced by the spirituality of martyrdom.[6]

As the early Church charismatic lifestyles began to disappear, the charismatic lifestyle that we call religious life began to emerge. Near the end of the third century, Christians withdrew into the desert to live a more intense Christian lifestyle. There were hermits, the most famous being Anthony, whose life was popularized in a biography written by Athanasius of Alexandria. Besides the single hermits, there were also groups of hermits ("lavrae") and cenobitic communities (common life). Not all individuals were suited for the solitary form of life and many of the hermits became eccentric. Communities developed, inspired by the communitarian image of the Acts of the Apostles. The communities also provided protection from the psychic, physical and spiritual hazards of the solitary life. The most noted of the cenobitic communities were those of Pachomius.

The ascetics of the desert went there as a radical human response to the religious dimension of life, desiring not to be passively guided and ruled by a decadent world. They revolted against the laxity of the Church at the end of the persecutions; they wanted to be true to themselves and to forget a world that divided them from themselves. The ascetics were seeking salvation in the desert, the classical place in the Judeo-Christian tradition to struggle with the devil and to find union with God.[7]

The men and women of the desert put a great deal of stress on asceticism: solitude, silence, and flight ("flee, be silent, be calm" — Arsenius).[8] They sought their true identity stripped of the illusions of the world. They put a great deal of emphasis on rest, quiet, contemplation, charity (especially hospitality and forgiveness), and practical wisdom.

The desert tradition spread rapidly in the East and West in the years that followed. It developed in Egypt, Palestine, Syria, Italy, and Gaul (France). Some of the great leaders among the men were Basil, Jerome, Evagrius, Cassian, Martin of Tours, Caesarius of Arles, and Augustine. The desert tradition spread even to Ireland, where it took on a particular Celtic form characterized by physical penances, a desire for exile, and a great love of nature and art (illumination such as the Book of Kells).

The desert movement was predominantly lay. Its prayers and liturgy were non-sacramental. Although there were priests who went to the desert, generally it was a movement separate from the clergy of the Church. When clergy were present, the ordained ministry was not necessarily emphasized. Palladius, for example, reports eight priests living at Nitria but only the senior priest celebrated the liturgy and preached.[9]   Anthony refused ordination. Cassian, in his *Institutes* (II, 18), apologized for his own ordination and encouraged the monk to flee the imposition of hands as contrary to the purpose of contemplation.[10]

The life of Pachomius, who went into hiding to avoid ordination, reflects an attitude of distance from the priesthood.[11]   In his biography, we read that Pachomius would invite a priest from the nearest churches to lead the celebration of liturgy, "for there was no one among them invested with the clerical office."[12] Pachomius believed "it was not good to ask for office and glory especially in a communal monastery, lest for that very reason strife and envy and jealousy and schisms arise among many monks . . . a clerical office is the beginning of contemplation of the lust for power."[13]   Despite these cautions, Pachomius was willing to accept a clergyman as a monk but that person was accepted in the same manner as all the other brothers.

There was a major exception to the attitude of caution and distance among the early ascetics. In Northern Africa at Hippo, Augustine merged the desert tradition of contemplation and asceticism with the life of the diocesan clergy. At first Augustine embraced the religious life in the desert tradition. After his return to Northern Africa from Italy, he set up a community of laymen dedicated to the contemplative life at Tagaste. He avoided trips to places where the bishop's chair was empty, fearing that he might be drafted into the ordained ministry. On one trip to Hippo, he was prevailed upon to be ordained a presbyter. Later, when the bishop died, he was chosen bishop and had to leave his lay community. Nevertheless, Augustine continued to live the contemplative life and encouraged his diocesan clergy to join him. He put a great emphasis on the common life. He changed the meaning of the word, "monk." For Augustine, the monk was not the solitary (one

alone) but the one in community (oneness of the common life).[14]
His brand of the ascetical vocation was a forerunner of the communities of canons regular in the Middle Ages which were founded
on his inspiration. According to Augustine, the contemplative life
was to be preferred,[15]   but it could be integrated into the service of
the ordained minister. Augustine viewed the lifestyle of contemplation as a significant addition to the life of an ordained minister.

The desert ascetics' attitude toward ordained ministry was
cautious and distant. The ascetics were predominantly lay people.
They felt that the life of ordained ministry would divert them from
the principal aim of religious life — the reign of God sought in
contemplation. They also felt that the introduction of ordained
ministry to their communities could lead to stratification, and be a
source of disharmony and dissension.

Monasticism

The Rise of the Monastic Movement

IN THE FIFTH CENTURY, a significant event for later religious
life took place in a monastery in Italy. Benedict of Nursia (c.480-
547) wrote a rule of life for a small community of monks at Monte
Cassino. His rule was to become the primary monastic rule of the
Middle Ages.

Benedict's rule was not original. It was based on earlier rules
such as the *Rule of the Master*. Its importance, however, arose
from its eminent wisdom and practicality. In a few pregnant
paragraphs, many found a fount of spiritual and human wisdom.
Benedict modeled his monastery on the concept of a family;
fraternal relationships among the members of the monastic community was key. Since the Roman model of family was the one
most familiar to Benedict, the role of the abbot as *paterfamilias*
was strong. The monastery was to be a school of discipline, a

school of love. To counteract a dangerous tendency among some of the desert ascetics, Benedict insisted on stability in one community as an important means to growth in the spiritual life. Mobility was seen as a physical manifestation of human pride and an unwillingness to enter the discipline of ascetical life.

Benedict's community was predominantly lay. The lifestyle was non-clerical; it was not centered on the Eucharist. De Vogüe concluded the following from his study of the Eucharist in Benedict's community: "At most it is possible that a conventual Mass in St. Benedict's monastery was celebrated on Sundays and feast days. But perhaps Mass was celebrated less often, even without fixed regularity."[16] The center of life was prayer (*Opus Dei* — what we would call the liturgy of the hours), lectio (reflective reading of Scripture and the desert fathers), and manual labor (mostly agricultural).

Benedict allowed clerics to enter the monastery but there was no mitigation of the rule or privileges granted to them. The priest took the place that corresponded to the date of his entry.[17] When calling a young man to ordination, the abbot was admonished to choose someone who was worthy.[18] The cleric monk was to be on guard against conceit or pride, was not to presume to do anything except what the abbot commanded him and was to recognize that now he would have to subject himself all the more to the discipline of the rule.[19]

Benedict shared the misgivings of the desert tradition about clerics in the monastery but he was more open to their presence than other monastic leaders like the author of the *Rule of the Master*.[20] There was no clerical apostolate for the monastery at Benedict's time. "The sole purpose of clerics in the monastery was to care for the sacramental needs of the community (and guests), and they were in no way to be exalted over the other monks."[21]

For Benedict, then, the ideal relationship between clerics and non-clerics in a monastery was fraternity. The clerics were to be servants and were to empty themselves of any of the privileges of the clerical state when they entered the monastery.

During the next few centuries, the *Rule of Benedict* became the most important monastic rule in Western Europe. At the request of Charlemagne and later his sons, Benedict of Aniane (751-821) made an effort to reform and unify monastic practice in the Empire. The *Rule of Benedict* became the rule for this short-lived reform. There were changes made, however, in Benedict's vision as the monks became involved in intellectual pursuits and a more ornate liturgy. The adoption of the feudal system led to less and less manual labor, which was now turned over to peasants who worked the monastic land. Because of new Eucharistic understandings (devotion to the real presence and private Masses) and missionary activity, Benedictine life became more clericalized. By the beginning of the 9th century, as many as 30% of monks were priests.[22] Daily Eucharist seemed to be a practice in most monasteries by the 10th century. An English document attests to two Masses a day.[23] With the breakup of the Carolingian Empire, many Benedictine houses became feudal property. Abbots often became vassals of territorial princes; generally there was a greater concern about monastic income than monastic spirituality. Monasticism went through a period of decline.

The Renewal of the Monastic Movement

During the 11th century, the Gregorian reform reached its peak in the Church. Among other things, it was a fight against secular influence in ecclesiatical administration. One goal of the reform was to strip civil, lay rulers of any jurisdiction in Church matters. As a structural response to the investiture conflict, it was successful. However, the elimination of lay jurisdiction in ecclesiastical affairs planted the seeds for a clericalization of the leadership of men's religious life in the centuries that followed.

There were two major renewal movements that revitalized monastic life and contributed to the rise of the Gregorian reform. In 909, a monastery was founded in France which had a tremendous influence on the Church during the succeeding years. The Abbot of Cluny was set up as a vassal of the bishop of Rome and was therefore free from any local control. The Abbey of Cluny began to thrive as a center of monastic life. During its years of glory (909-1109), it led a monastic family with close to 2,000 houses subject to it. The monastic ''chapel'' at Cluny was the largest church in Christendom (when St. Peter's in Rome was rebuilt in the 16th century, it was planned a few feet longer than Cluny's monastic church). During the reform of the papacy (1073-1119), six monks occupied the papal throne, at least three coming from Cluniac monasteries.

Monastic life at Cluny was highly clericalized. By the 12th century, almost all monks were ordained. The celebration of an ornate liturgy and the proliferation of intercessory masses emphasized the importance of the clerical monk over the lay monk. Much of the work on the land was done by lay servants.

A second significant renewal movement, which took place in the 12th century as a counterpoint to Cluny, had a significant influence on the relationship between clerics and non-clerics in religious life. In 1098, after several previous attempts, Robert, abbot of Molesme, became a hermit with several companions at Citeaux. He and his companions had a ''dream of seclusion and poverty, a life unhampered by worldly cares and dedicated to God's service alone.''[24] After a year, Robert returned to Molesme to resume the office of abbot. Alberic, who then became abbot of Citeaux, and his successor as abbot, Stephen Harding, set up statutes intended to enforce the Benedictine rule in its primitive form. The new foundation (the beginning of the order known today as the Cistercians) had a major effect on religious life development. At the height of its growth in the 13th century, the Cistercian order had over 700 houses.

The aim of the Cistercians was solitude and poverty, a more faithful living of the *Rule of Benedict*. They wanted to be separated from the world and from the spirit of material gain. The liturgy of the monastery was simplified. The Cistercians refused feudal and economic ties with society. Manual labor was restored and, in general, servants were not hired. The Cistercians wanted their monasteries to be economically independent. Therefore, they adopted and expanded an idea that had surfaced in some other recent monastic reforms (e.g., Vallombrosa), the creation of a class of lay brothers (*conversi*).

The lay brothers were employed to assist the choir monks in manual labor and save the choir monks from the distraction of temporal business. Often a Cistercian monastery developed fields far from the monastery itself, making it difficult to return for prayer. The lay brothers farmed these granges and often stayed there. Since the lay brothers were mostly unlettered and simple people, they had a simple form of prayer based on the recitation of the Lord's Prayer and the Hail Mary. Although they did make a monastic type of profession, they could not become monks or priests.

Unprecedented numbers joined the Cistercians as lay brothers. Some abbeys had as many as 350 lay brothers. According to the biographer of Abbot Aelred, there were 500 lay brothers and 140 choir monks at Rievaulx at the time of the abbot's death.[25]   In the early 13th century, it is estimated that there were 3,200 lay brothers in England and Wales alone.[26]   The desire to escape poverty and insecurity by entering a great and prosperous abbey was a powerful incentive in a majority of applications.[27]   This motivation was not, however, always conducive to monastic regularity.

At first it appears that most of the lay brothers observed the rules prescribed for them. Many, including some from noble families, were held in high esteem. However, as Lekai indicates, the physical separation of the lay brothers (on the granges) from the monks (in the monasteries) "accentuated by theoretical and legal considerations, reintroduced between the two groups the servant-master relationship, the very thing earlier generations had tried to avoid. In 1188 the General chapter passed a statute demanding that 'noble laymen coming to our monasteries should become monks and not *conversi.*' "[28]   It appears that a noble would disgrace his peers by becoming a lay brother. By the end of the 12th century, in the general chapter documentation of the Cistercian order, references are found to revolts by the lay brothers. In fact there are records of 123 serious disturbances by lay brothers between 1190-1300.[29]   These records of the revolts are recorded by the abbots gathered in Chapter and therefore show the perspective of the abbots rather than the lay brothers themselves. But it is clear that there was antagonism between the lay brothers and the monks. This led to the prohibition of the lay brothers' voting in the election of the abbot, the prohibition of wine and beer on the granges, and the eventual prohibition of the acceptance of new lay brothers in monasteries that had difficulties with them. Eventually the lay brothers in many Cistercian monasteries were replaced by lay people who leased the land (the very practice the Cistercians had tried to avoid).

The relationship between the monks (mostly clerics) and the lay brothers was not fraternal. There were clear signs of antagonism. Clearly, there were instances of violence on the part of the lay brothers. There were also extreme disciplinary measures used by the abbots and monks on the lay brothers, some of which would appear discriminatory. Although the prohibition against beer and wine on the granges was enacted to end inappropriate behavior there, this prohibition appeared discriminatory to some of the lay brothers, since beer and wine were not forbidden in the abbey. After the 13th century, the number of lay brothers declined because of the change of the Cistercian economic system, the hostility toward the lay brothers in the order, and the attraction of the new religious movements.[30]   The relationship between clerics and non-clerics in the Cistercian order was then not a happy one. Abuses of power on both sides led many times to an adversarial relationship. As the Cistercian monks became involved in study and education, there was less time for manual labor. The development of a stratification in Cistercian communities led to a servant-master relationship between clerics and non-clerics.

During the 12th and 13th centuries, monastic life again declined. Monasteries became wealthy. With the rise of the mendicant orders, many of the most spiritually and mentally gifted chose that form of life over the monastic life. At the same time the clericalization of monastic orders was completed. This can be seen in the action of the Council of Vienne in 1311 which prescribed that monks have the duty to allow themselves to be ordained.[31]

Although the monastic movement dominated the early Medieval Church, there were other developments in religious life. The integration of clerical pastoral duties and religious life, which first appeared with St. Augustine, flowered again in the 12th and 13th centuries in the development of the canons regular. The two predominant groups were the Canons Regular of St. Augustine (the Austin Canons or the black canons) and the Premonstratensians (Norbertines, Canons Regular of Premontre, or the white canons). These groups blended the monastic community life with an active life of preaching and pastoral work.

Another more short-lived development also took place at this time. During the crusades to protect the Holy Land, the military and ransom orders developed as a unique form of religious life in the 11th-13th centuries. Some of these orders had priests and lay religious (e.g. knights and nurses). In general, they did not have a lasting impact on religious life. Some of these orders were suppressed (e.g., the Templars), some went out of existence (e.g., the Antoines, the Hospitalers of the Holy Spirit), and some were substantially changed by later movements, especially the mendicant movement (e.g., the Trinitarians, the Mercedarians).

Mendicant Orders

DURING THE 13TH CENTURY there was a search for a new world order. Mobile wealth was becoming more important than landed wealth; trade and money were displacing agriculture as the basis for the economy. There was movement from a rural agrarian culture to an urban commercial culture. The merchant class was growing. The spiritual response to this movement was evangelical poverty. There was a variety of movements that incorporated this value, many of which developed heretical branches (e.g., the Humiliati, the Cathari, and the Waldensians). The medicant religious orders provided an effective alternative to the heretical movements. The best known of these orders are the Franciscans and the Dominicans. The other major groups are the Augustinians, the Carmelites, and the Servites. Expansion was rapid. By 1325, for example, there were over 70,000 members of the mendicant orders.[32]

Although as mendicant orders the Dominicans and the Franciscans have some similarities in their spiritualities, they differ in their development concerning the relationship between clerical and non-clerical members in their midst.

The Dominicans were founded as an order of preachers. Dominic, at the request of Innocent III, adopted one of the ancient rules of the Church, the rule of St. Augustine, and thereby aligned his order in the tradition of the canons regular rather than the monastic orders. Dominic did not want the members of the order to be involved in manual labor. They were to have the intellectual training to support the preaching mission that was given to them. Dominic did accept lay brothers, *conversi*, in the order to do domestic and manual work. They shared in the life of the priest members in the chapel, in the refectory, and in the dormitory. They attended choir at the same hours, but silently recited their *Paters* and *Aves* while the friars chanted the Divine Office. However, there were certain prohibitions. They could not hold certain offices, they could not pass to the clerical state and they could not do certain kinds of studies.

The Franciscans, on the other hand, emerged from the penitential movement of the early 13th century (a lay movement). Francis founded a brotherhood that was at first predominantly lay. Fraternity among the brothers was a key point in their life. Thomas Celano, one of the early biographers of Francis, wrote: "There was indeed at that time a great rejoicing and a singular joy among St. Francis and his brothers whenever one of the faithful, no matter what his status might be, rich or poor, of high or low birth, of lowly regard or high esteem, prudent or simple, cleric or unlettered or a layman from among the Christian people, led on by the Holy Spirit of God, came to put on the habit of holy religious."[33]   The original intent of the fraternity was to live the Gospel and to preach a simple message of repentance.

The fraternity of the early Franciscans, expressed in the equality between clerics and non-clerics, was up against a clerical culture in the Church which would make it difficult to sustain. In the early 13th century, Innocent III insisted that laymen, even if they were religious, should not be given any authority over churches or ecclesiatical persons.[34]   The Fourth Lateran Council restricted all preaching to clerics.[35]   In this context the Franciscan order began the rapid process of clericalization and the loss of the fraternal equality that characterized the early brotherhood. This clericalization was the result of two forces. One was an external force — the call of the Church through the Fourth Lateran Council and the decrees of the Popes to a preaching mission and the hearing of confessions of the laity, a clerical apostolate.[36]   An internal force in the clericalization process came from the clerics who lived within the order. They were recruited from a Church that was highly clerical. Their desire to clericalize the order was fueled when abuses developed during the generalate of Elias, a layman.[37]   During the generalate of Haymo of Faversham (1240-1244), legislation was enacted which disqualified laymen for the office of superior whenever priests were available to serve. Most probably it was under Haymo that certain restrictions on the admission of laymen were enacted.[38]   Francis founded his fraternity in 1211. The original twelve may all have been laymen. By 1260, the clerics in the order superseded the lay members both in numbers and in importance.

The clericalization of the Franciscans destroyed that equality and fraternity experienced at the beginning. In the canon law of the time, clerics were considered nobler than laity. This law was preoccupied with the rights, privileges, and obligations of the clerics. Laymen were considered inferior to clerics and were somewhat negatively viewed. It is not surprising, then, that some clerics in the Franciscans began to view the laymembers as their servants.[39]

Another mendicant order, the Augustinians, began developing in 1243-1244, as the result of a number of hermits asking of the Holy See permission to adopt the rule and style of life of St. Augustine (The Little Union). Later the order expanded with the merger of other orders in the Great Union of 1256. At the time of the Great Union, a majority of Augustinians were probably laymen. The percentage of priests increased rapidly, however, with the emphasis on studies and the apostolate of the mendicants (urged on the order by the Church), which was chiefly pastoral. Many of the basic elements of Augustinian life were shared equally by all the brothers, both clerical and lay. At the beginning the lay brothers, *conversi*, had some voice in government. They could not, however, be elected to provincial chapters or general chapters. Since the major superiors were elected from these chapters, it followed that they could not be major superiors. Although the Augustinians have as an end the promotion of unity in charity by means of community, their fraternity was influenced by the prevailing practice in the Church and the practice of the two major mendicant orders. Although in the earliest days the lay brothers participated in the life of the community, they were slowly relegated to a servant-type role as they were excluded from leadership positions.[40]

In summary, the relations between laymen and clerics in mendicant religious life went through a profound shift. The Franciscans and Augustinians started with an experience of equality and fraternity. Historical events, theological interpretations, and the stratified Church culture of the day led to a situation where clerics were considered superior to lay brothers, the latter often being relegated to the role of servant. A similar experience seems to have transpired within the Servites and the Carmelites.[41]   This stratification destroyed one of the great gifts of the early mendicant movement and led to a gulf between clerics and non-clerics that has existed to some extent down to our own day. With the reform of the Second Vatican Council, the mendicant orders have begun the process of rediscovering their original charism and examining the relationship between clerical and non-clerical members.

Apostolic Orders

IN THE 14TH AND 15TH CENTURIES, religious life entered another era of decline. Religious life and the Church were affected by the Hundred Year's War, the Avignon Papacy, the Great Schism, the corruption of the Roman curia and the lower clergy, the Renaissance papacy, and the Black Death. The mendicant orders so popular in the 13th century were somewhat corrupted by their own success.

One movement of this period was the spiritual movement called "devotio moderna," best known for the book, *The Imitation of Christ*, written by Thomas â Kempis. This movement sprung from the Brothers and Sisters of the Common Life founded by Gerard Groote (1340-1384). In one of his foundations, Groote set up a form of common life at the vicarage of St. Paul's in Deventer (Holland). Lay people and clergy lived together a life of service and prayer. There were, however, no binding vows (a reaction to the formalism and lack of devotion among the religious of the time). The promise which the movement might have had to revitalize religious life and to reestablish a community in which clerics and non-clerics would live in harmonious union was wiped out with the advent of the Protestant Reformation in the 16th century. The "devotio moderna" (centered in Northern Europe) lost its strength at that time.

The Counter-Reformation included a reform of religious life and the advent of new forms. For some men religious, these new forms were mostly all clerical. The Theatines, Somaschi, Barnabites, and Piarists, for example were all founded at this time. The Jesuit order was the largest of these new apostolic orders of priests. "The Society of Jesus was founded principally for the defense and propagation of the faith and for the rendering of any service in the Church that may be for the glory of God and the common good."[42] The spirit of the Jesuits flowed from the needs of the Church in the Counter-Reformation period; the Church needed educated clergy to reform itself and challenge the errors of its adversaries.

The Society of Jesus began as a society of priests. Pope Paul III permitted the acceptance of spiritual (priests) and temporal (lay brothers) coadjutors who were not solemnly professed members of the Society.[43]   Although the Society included all the members under obedience to the superior general, the Society did have different grades: professed, spiritual and temporal coadjutors, and scholastics.[44]   In the mind of Ignatius, to be a coadjutor (a helper) was a great privilege since service of God and neighbor was a great Christian virtue. He therefore wrote of the coadjutors: "They should be content with their grade, knowing that in the eyes of our Creator and Lord those gain greater merit who with greater charity give help and service to all persons through love of His Divine Majesty, whether they serve in matters of greater moment or in others more lowly and humble."[45]   The temporal coadjutor was to have the lot of Martha; he was involved in occupations such as cook, steward, buyer, doorkeeper, and similar duties.[46]

Although, in the mind of Ignatius, all members were equal, some organizational expressions led to the impression that temporal coadjutors were second class citizens in the Society. For example, although the spiritual and temporal coadjutors were to consider themselves perpetually dedicated to God, the Society through the Superior could dismiss the coadjutor at any time.[47] The inequality of temporal coadjutors was expressed in another way. For Ignatius the discernment of one's place in the Society was a very important discernment. Once a member was accepted into the Society in one grade, however, he was not to seek to pass into another. Flowing from this, the temporal coadjutor was not "to seek more learning than he had when he entered."[48]   This was in line with Ignatius' principle that, if one had properly discerned one's vocation, then one should not strive to change one's vocation. Later this principle of Ignatius was to be given a stricter interpretation. "Let no one of those admitted for domestic services learn either to read or write, or, if he has any knowledge of letters, acquire more; and let no one teach him without leave of the General; but it shall be sufficient for him to serve Christ Our Lord with holy simplicity and humility."[49]

In the early days of the Society of Jesus, there were no rules of division requiring priests, scholastics, and brothers to live and recreate apart in separated groups. Slowly through the passage of time further distinctions were made. "Often permissions thought ordinary for priests or scholastics were thought extraordinary for brothers; and, by our twentieth century, class-consciousness was rising among many brothers who felt themselves to be 'second-class citizens.' "[50]

Although today we would see an inequality expressed in the various grades in the Jesuit order, it must be remembered that the Society of Jesus arose within a cultural context which was stratified and in which clerics in the Church were considered superior to laymen. Clearly today this approach has been challenged. In the wake of the Second Vatican Council, the Jesuits have begun to rethink the role of the temporal coadjutor. A downward trend in the number of brothers' vocations has helped spur this rethinking.[51] We will return to this story in the final section of this chapter.

Age of Institutional Ministries

IN THE 17TH AND 18TH CENTURIES, the Church and religious life faced the increasing secularization of culture and the rise of nationalism. There was more control exerted on religious orders by the states. Some orders were banished or suppressed. In 1766, for example, a Commission of Regulars was set up in France that secularized nine Congregations and closed more than 400 religious houses.[52]   From 1759-1768, the Jesuits were slowly expelled from Latin countries and colonies. Finally in 1773, Clement XIV, under political pressure, suppressed the order completely, although the suppression was not totally effective.

During this time there were reform movements in the traditional orders and the rise of new religious orders. The French School of Spirituality had a major influence on religious life. Leaders of this school founded religious societies of priests. The French Oratory (Peter de Berulle), the Congregation of the Mission also known as the Vincentians (St. Vincent de Paul), the Sulpicians (Jean Jacques Olier), the Apostolic Missionaries of Jesus and Mary (John Eudes), and similar groups, were involved in pastoral ministry: reform of the clergy, preaching missions, foreign missions, and training of priests. These groups were predominantly societies of priests with simple and private vows. Two religious congregations with preaching apostolates (the Passionists and the Redemptorists) were founded in the early 18th century. These orders were predominantly clerical and drew heavily upon the

French School of Spirituality's great reverence for the dignity of the priesthood.

A harbinger of things to come also appeared during the late 17th and early 18th centuries, the foundation of totally lay congregations dedicated to institutional ministries. The Christian Brothers (1681) and the Brothers of Christian Instruction (1709) are probably the best known. John Baptist de La Salle, who founded the Institute of the Brothers of the Christian Schools (Christian Brothers), wanted the members to have religious vows, a common life, an exclusively educational apostolate (especially education of the poor), and an exclusively lay character.[53] This last characteristic resulted from an unfortunate encounter which illustrated the clericalism of the times. De La Salle resigned as superior of his community and Bro. Henri L'Heureux was chosen as his successor. The Archbishop of Rheims, deeming it unbecoming for a priest to be subject to a layman, annulled the election. De La Salle then proposed that Bro. Henri prepare for the priesthood. During his studies, he died. De La Salle took this as a sign from God that the members of the order should not be ordained. Later another brother was elected as superior to replace De La Salle. To avoid the clericalism of the time and to protect their educational apostolate De La Salle finally decided that the order should remain totally lay.

With the dawn of the nineteenth century, religious life, in general, faced a major crisis brought on by anticlericalism, the distrust of religious evidenced in most writers of the Age of Enlightenment, the suppression of houses and persecutions of religious, and by the decadence of many religious and religious houses. On the eve of the French Revolution there were over 300,000 men religious. After the revolution and secularization there were 70,000.[54]   However, the crisis led to a new ferment and the growth of new religious congregations. During the 19th century, there were over 600 new communities founded, 91 of which were pontifical foundations of men. Most of the new congregations were from France and Germany. The older orders also underwent a renewal. Religious responded to the needs of the times and became involved in institutional apostolates such as schools, hospitals, and orphanages.

Most orders of men continued to be either clerical or totally lay. The spirit of the French revolution (liberty, equality, and fraternity) led some founders to attempt new forms of relationships between clerics and non-clerics. There were several attempts to set up religious orders where clerics and non-clerics lived in equality. Two examples of this approach were the Society of Mary (Marianists) and the Congregation of Holy Cross.

The Society of Mary (Marianists), founded in 1817 by Father William Joseph Chaminade, was started as a congregation of mixed composition (priests and lay members) much like the Society of Bordeaux from which it sprang. Chaminade wanted his institute to mirror the original community of Jerusalem and the family of Benedict. The priest members were to be primarily of service to their brothers. Early in the Society's existence the separation of the priests and lay religious was suggested but Father Chaminade held firm to the conviction of keeping them together. He wanted the Society to be what the Church should be, clerics and non-clerics in a community of one mind and one heart. During its subsequent history there was a crisis at the time of the approbation of the constitutions in 1865. Among the 40 animadversions that Rome made to the text submitted for approval, was a requirement that only priests be directors of communities. There was an outcry in the Society, many feeling that the original spirit was in jeopardy. Some suggested separation into two religious institutes. This led to the appointment of an apostolic visitor. In his interviews with the members, the visitor, Cardinal Mathieu, determined that the members overwhelmingly favored keeping the Society united rather than separating into a society of priest and a society of lay brothers. The Society remained, then, a community of priests and lay members. Certain offices, however, were restricted to priest members. The structuring of the relationship of equality and complementarity among the members of the Society has been an important focus of the Society up to the present. The renewal of the Second Vatican Council led the Society to examine these structures again.

The Congregation of Holy Cross developed a different structure of relationship between clerical and non-clerical members. The initial inspiration of Basil Moreau was to have a religious congregation of three societies — one of priests, a second of lay men religious and a third of women religious — "working in close collaboration on an equal footing."[55]   He decided on a structure in which each group had a separate government under a single general chapter and general administration. As Thomas Barrosse, CSC, has pointed out, Moreau was probably aware "of difficulties of assuring a collaboration of equals in a world dominated by men and a Church governed exclusively by clerics."[56]   Pope Pius IX refused to approve the women as part of the same congregation as the men. In 1855, the general chapter suppressed the independent government for the priests and brothers and set up mixed provinces. Only the office of superior general was reserved to the priests. Later, the office of provincial was limited to the priests in response to the demands made by the codification of canon law in 1917. Still, the attitude of equality and fraternity was to be the hallmark of the institute: "Worthy of praise is this institute made up of priests and laymen so joined together in friendly alliance that, while the nature of each society is preserved, neither prevails over the other, but both cooperate in the best possible way in realizing the respective ends."[57]

In 1945 the general chapter reversed the earlier decision of mixed provinces. The mixed provinces had not assured the cooperation and equality in the founder's vision. The decision of the chapter was to restructure the institute into separate provinces some of priests and others of brothers. A priest, however, could live in a house directed by a brother and a brother in a house directed by a priest. A class distinction was added by the Sacred Congregation of Religious. The brothers in manual labor who joined a priests' province were deprived of the right of active and passive voice in government.[58]

The 1917 codification of canon law did not break any new ground in the relationship between clerics and non-clerical members in religious institutes. In most cases, it solidified the status quo. Distinctions were codified. For example, the formation of clerics and lay brothers was separated; the formation for one class did not qualify for that of the other.[59] The codification did not recognize mixed institutes. Institutes were either clerical or lay.[60] Clerical institutes took precedence over lay institutes. [61] In those determined to be clerical, non-clerical members were not given an equal participation in the government. There were few changes in the relationship between clerics and non-clerics in religious institutes during the 20th century until the call of the Second Vatican Council for institutes to renew themselves in the light of the gospels, the founding charism, and the signs of the time.

In the relationship between clerics and non-clerics, each of the criterion for renewal of the Second Vatican Council raised questions for religious institutes. The gospel of Jesus challenged the structural relationships that embodied privileges for some members of an institute not given to others. Reflection on the inspiration and the charism of the founder has led many institutes to re-examine the structures adopted from culture and the Church which may have blunted the strength of the original inspiration. Finally, reflecting on the signs of the times, especially the growth of the democratic spirit in the past two hundred years and the unprecedented education of lay people in the Church, religious men have examined carefully hierarchical structures adopted from earlier cultures.

The renewal has happened in different ways and will lead to further change in the future. The Congregation of Religious and Secular Institutes recently studied the subject at a Plenaria in 1986. Many monastic communities have returned to the concept of one monastic profession. In the rewriting of the *Rule of Life*, the Society of Mary (Marianists) has opened the office of provincial to both priests and lay members. At its most recent general chapter, a proposal was made to open all positions including superior general to both clerical and lay members. Although not passed, it will most likely appear again at a future chapter. The Congregation of Holy Cross made a similar proposal to the Congregation of Religious and Secular Institutes at the time it submitted its revised rule for approbation. It wished all offices to be opened to all members both clerical and lay. The Congregation of Religious denied the request but left the door open for possible change in the future.[62]

The Jesuits faced the issue at their XXXII Congregation in 1974-1975. There was a strong desire among many in the order for the abolition of grades and the admission of all Jesuits to the four solemn vows, including those who were not priests. Cardinal Villot, in a letter addressed to the Congregation, expressed the concern of the Holy See that this would be contrary to the charism of the foundation.[63]   The Jesuits decided to take up the issue and after further discernment to resubmit the issue to the Holy Father. The Holy Father asked the Congregation to take no further action in the issue and reaffirmed his belief that he could not grant a change in this matter.[64]   The Congregation did call for a strengthening of the unity of vocation of all the members of whatever grade.[65]   This call to unity has its obstacles. One Jesuit expressed it well. His comments may speak to situations in other institutes where inequality has existed between clerics and non-clerics:

> The greatest obstacle to the sharing in *koinonia* is a lack of simplicity and frankness in our dealings with one another. This is especially true when the Brothers are involved. Sometimes the fault is on the side of the Brothers, who perhaps nurse hurts caused by real or imagined slights received in the past from priests and scholastics. Other times, the fault is on the side of the priests who patronize the Brothers and talk down to them, or think that only trivial matters are fit subjects of discussion with them.[66]

The Second Vatican Council declared that there was no objection to religious congregations of brothers admitting some members to holy orders to supply needed priestly ministration for their own houses and works. Some groups like the Brothers of the Sacred Heart have taken advantage of this openness. They see the priestly ministry by some of their brothers as serving the particular charism of their institute especially in areas where there is a lack of priest ministers.[67]

Another lay order, the Christian Brothers, has decided not to ordain brothers to the priestly ministry. Some in the order have expressed the concern that ordained ministry might endanger the exclusively educational apostolate and the lay character of the institute.[68] Some have wondered if the desire for priesthood might not be evidence of a lack of understanding and appreciation for the lay vocation.[69] Finally, in a survey done to determine opinion among the members, a subtle anti-clericalism was discovered that might make it difficult for priest members to function.

> When asked whether there is a clerical mentality different from the
> community spirit of the brothers, almost to a man the answer was
> yes, and that mentality was characterized in the following ways:
> Priests have a superiority complex, they think themselves special
> and apart from everyone else because they feel they have sacred
> powers; they're hampered by legalism; they live in a closed world
> advocating the status quo; they have no sense of simplicity and hard
> work; they're much too independent; though some might be saintly,
> many have a crude arrogance; they're so authority conscious that
> hierarchical considerations are more important than ministry;
> they're climbers in ecclesiastical structures; they're so concerned
> about structures they forget about people and community.[70]

We are, then, in a period of profound transition. The relationship of clerics and non-clerics in religious institutes is an important part of that transition in the image of the religious life. The Second Vatican Council has challenged each institute to renewal that may challenge present structures.

Conclusions

AT THE BEGINNING of this chapter on the history of the relationship between clerics and non-clerics in men's religious institutes, we said that the study of history will hopefully free us from the illusion that present practice is the norm for the Church in all ages. As we have seen, the relationship between clerics and non-clerics has changed over the ages and in the inspiration of different institutes. We are called to be open to the Spirit of God as we grapple with the structures of religious life today.

I believe the study of history gives us some direction in our present day discernment. Some of the questions that might be raised as a result of the study of history are the following:

1. Does the New Testament message about a community of one mind and one heart call for each community to examine any community structures that give privileges to one group in the institute?

2. In institutes which are presently clerical, is this clerical orientation an accident of history or is it an essential part of the institute's identity? As the Church rethinks the ordained ministry, will religious institutes need to rethink their structures? If preaching, for example, would not be limited to clerics in the future, would an order with a preaching apostolate need to keep the clerical state as an essential part of its charism?

3. In an age of educated laity, do the structures that emerged in an age of illiterate laity still make sense? Has the Church come to an appreciation of an educated laity?

4. Does the division of the Church into two groups, "clergy" and "laity," make sense any more? Do we need new categories of thought and expression?

5. With the breakdown of class privilege and the growing democratic spirit of the past two hundred years (since the French and American revolutions), are religious not challenged by the Spirit in our times to eliminate class distinctions and promote the dignity of each member?

6. Do the religious of today need to manifest a lifestyle that challenges and balances the hierarchical model of Church that is present in diocesan and parochial structures?

7. Does the history of religious life challenge the present codification of Church law to recognize not only lay and clerical institutes but true mixed institutes which are not intended to favor either the clerical or lay state?

8. Does not history teach us that orders which are totally lay need to be careful not to develop a subtle anti-clericalism and orders that are totally clerical need to be careful not to develop a mentality of clerical superiority?

A time of transition is a difficult time. Tension becomes a part of life. A time of transition, however, is also a marvelous opportunity to reshape our response of faith to our world. The future of religious life (its renewal and growth) demands that we be people of faith just as the people who have gone before us were faithful to the Spirit calling them in their times. Dominic, Benedict, Francis, Ignatius, De La Salle, and other founders never lived to see the great religious families that resulted from their work. We will probably not see the flowering of the new age of religious life. But we are still called to be people of faith; to believe that a new age is dawning; to believe that Christ is still with us until the end of time.

Endnotes

1 Second Vatican Council, *Lumen Gentium*, paragraph 43.

2 John Lozano, *Life as Parable* (New York: Paulist Press, 1986).

3 James Fitz, "Religious Life as Acted Prophecy" *Review for Religious*. 41:6 (November-December, 1982), p. 923-927.

4 The 1983 Code of Canon Law, c. 573.

5 Larry Cada and Raymond Fitz, "The Recovery of Religious Life" *Review for Religious*. 34:5 (September, 1975), p. 690-718. This article later appeared in a revised form in the book, Larry Cada, et al. *Shaping the Coming Age of Religious Life* (New York: The Seabury Press, 1979).

6 The language used to describe martyrdom in the works of Cyprian, Tertullian, Origen, Augustine and other early Church writers is often picked up by later writers in describing religious life.

7 Thomas Merton, *The Wisdom of the Desert* (New York: New Directions, 1970), especially p. 3-24.

8 Thomas Merton, *Contemplation in a World of Action* (Garden City, New York: Image Books, 1973), p. 285-286. See also Henri J.M. Nouwen, *The Way of the Heart* (New York: The Seabury Press, 1981), p. 15.

9 Palladius, *The Lausiac History*, Ancient Christian Writers, No. 34, translated and edited by Robert T. Meyer (Westminster, Maryland: The Newman Press, 1965), p. 41.

10 John Cassian, *Conferences* translated and preface by Colm Luibheid, introduction by Owen Chadwick (New York: Paulist Press, 1985), p. 30. See also Claude Peifer *Monastic Spirituality* (New York: Sheed and Ward, 1966), p. 329.

11 *The Life of Pachomius (Vita Prima Graeca)* translated by Apostolos N. Athanassakis, (Missoula, Montana: Scholars Press, 1975), paragraph 30 (p. 41).

12 Ibid., paragraph 27 (p. 35).

13 Ibid.

14 Augustine, Commentary on Psalm 133 (134).

15 Augustine, *De Quantitate Animae*.

16 De Vogue is quoted in *RB 1980, The Rule of St. Benedict*, edited by Timothy Fray (Collegeville, Minnesota: The Liturgical Press, 1981), p. 412.

17 The Rule of Benedict, chapter 60.

18 Ibid., chapter 62.

19 Ibid.

20 The Rule of the Master, chapter 83.

21 *RB 1980*, p. 96.

22 Lawrence Landini, *Causes of Clericalization of the Friars Minor 1209-1260 in the Light of Early Franciscan Sources*, (Chicago: Dissertatio ad Lauream in Facultate Historiae Ecclesiasticae Pontificiae Universitatis Gregorianae, 1968), page 13. Landini quotes figures from Otto Nussbaum.

23 R. Kevin Seasoltz, "Monastery and Eucharist: Some American Observations" *The Continuing Quest for God* (Collegeville, Minnesota: The Liturgical Press, 1982), p. 223.

24 Louis J. Lekai, *The Cistercians, Ideals and Reality* (Kent, Ohio: Kent State University Press, 1977), p. 12.
25 C.H. Lawrence, *Medieval Monasticism*, (London and New York: Longman, 1984), p. 149.
26 Lekai, p. 337-338.
27 Ibid.
28 Ibid., p. 340.
29 James S. Donnelly, *The Decline of the Medieval Cistercian Laybrotherhood* (New York: Fordham University Press, 1949), especially p. 71-80.
30 Ibid., especially p. 70.
31 Francois Vandenbroucke, *Why Monk?* translated by Leon Brockman, OCSO, (Washington, D.C.: Cistercian Publications, Consortium Press, 1972), p. 86-87.
32 Cada et al., *Shaping*, p. 30.
33 Quoted from Thomas Celano's *First Life* of St. Francis (Part I, Book 1, Chapter 12, paragraph 31) by Landini, p. 26.
34 Landini, p. 15, 123.
35 By 1240 the mind of the Church was against lay persons preaching any type of sermons, even the call of penance granted to the first friars, ibid., p. 111.
36 Ibid., p. 142-144.
37 Ibid., p. 123, 144.
38 Ibid., p. 143.
39 Ibid., p. 140.
40 Cyril Counihan, "Lay and Clerical Elements in Early Augustinian History" *Anallecta Augustiana*. 43 (1980), 305-333.
41 Giancarlo Rocca "Fathers and Brothers in Religious Institutes" *Brothers in Our Institutes*, Proceedings of the XXXI Meeting of the Union of Superiors General, Villa Cavalletti, May 22-25, 1985, pp. 10-11.
42 *Documents of the 31st and 32nd General Congregation of the Society of Jesus.* (St. Louis, Missouri: The Institute of Jesuit Sources, 1977), p. 403.
43 George E. Ganss, "The Jesuit Brother's Vocation" *The Jesuit Brothers' Vocation* (Rome, Italy: Centrum Ignatianum Spiritualitatis, 1983), p. 21.
44 Ibid., pp. 22-23; see also *The Constitutions of the Society of Jesus* translated, with an introduction and a commentary by George E. Ganss (St. Louis: The Institute of Jesuit Resources, 1970), p. 82-83.
45 Ibid., p. 32, see also *Constitutions*, p. 114.
46 Ibid., p. 39; see also *Constitutions*, p. 128.
47 Ibid., p. 29; see also *Constitutions*, p. 114.
48 Ibid., p. 37.
49 Ibid., pp. 54-58.
50 Ibid., p. 50.
51 *The Jesuit Brother: A Statement by the National Jesuit Brothers' Committee to American Jesuits*, p. 2.
52 Lekai, p. 162.

53 Thomas Michael Loome, "Concerning the Ordination to the Priesthood of Members of the Institute of the Brothers of the Christian Schools," *Priestly Brothers* (Winona, Minnesota: St. Mary's College Press, 1975), pp. 20-21.

54 Cada et al., *Shaping*, p. 38.

55 Thomas Barrosse, "The Experience of Holy Cross," Proceedings of the XXXI Meeting of the Union of Superiors General, Villa Cavalletti, May 22-25, 1985, p. 60.

56 Ibid.

57 Ibid., p. 61.

58 Ibid., p. 62.

59 The 1917 Code of Canon Law, canons 558, 564:2.

60 Ibid., canon 488.

61 Ibid., canon 491.

62 Barrosse, p. 62.

63 *Documents*, p. 373.

64 Ibid., p. 374.

65 Ibid., p. 375.

66 Thomas H. Clancy, "Simplicity and Frankness" *The Jesuit Brothers' Vocation* (Rome, Italy: Centrum Ignatianum Spiritualitatis, 1983), p. 115.

67 Jean-Charles Daigneault, "The Ordained Brother in the Institute of the Brothers of the Sacred Heart," Proceedings of the XXXI Meeting of the Union of Superiors General, Villa Cavalletti, May 22-25, 1985, p. 82.

68 Loome, pp. 20-21.

69 Martin Helldorfer, "Priestly Brothers?" *Priestly Brothers?* (Winona, Minnesota: St. Mary's College Press, 1975), pp. 30-32.

70 William Mueller, "Brotherhood-Priesthood" *Priestly Brothers?* (Winona, Minnesota: St. Mary's College Press, 1975), pp. 33-34.

Cultural Context for Current Relationships

REV. ROBERT J. SCHREITER, C.PP.S.

The Impact of Culture on
Brother-Priest Relations

THERE ARE MANY THINGS which work together in shaping the relations between brothers and priests in religious institutes. Most often dwelt upon in any analysis of those relations are the historical and theological ones, i.e., those growing out of the lived experience and the lore of an institute, and those reflecting the evangelical and theological ideals of that institute.

Most people are at least vaguely aware that other factors also shape these relations: class and ethnic background, specific apostolate undertaken by the institute, and so on. This chapter dwells on one of those other factors which, while evident in a variety of ways, often remains elusive in an analysis of how brothers and priests relate both within the community and in their ministries.

What will be explored here is one of those pervasive yet hard to grasp factors, namely, the role culture plays in giving shape to how members of a religious institute relate to each other. This factor is a pervasive one because all humans live in at least one kind of culture or another. Culture as a factor in human relations is hard to grasp precisely because of its pervasive character, and especially when it is the culture of which we are a part. Culture is something like the air we breathe: we only really notice it when it does not seem to be quite in order or seems to have left us altogether.

Culture as a concept is notoriously hard to define. There is no general agreement among students of culture just how to understand this concept. In order to provide some focus for the presentation here, some distinctions and a definition can be of help.

First of all, the emphasis here will be on the broad aspects of culture: how people in a given situation understand themselves, their relations, and their ideals. This is in contrast to understanding culture primarily as what is sometimes called "high culture" or the artistic products of a people — their art, music, literature and so on. While the products of high culture will not be excluded here, emphasis will be more on the day-to-day interactions within a people.

Secondly, emphasis will be on the symbolic products rather than the material products of a culture. That is to say, the focus will be upon the value (both stated and implied), the ideals, and the meanings which a people assign to aspects of their environment. This is done in contrast to looking at the material achievements of that people.

With these two distinctions in mind, we can give a working definition of culture, borrowed from the anthropologist Clifford Geertz:

> (Culture) denotes an historically transmitted pattern of meanings embodied in symbols, a system of inherited conceptions expressed in symbolic forms by which men communicate, perpetuate, and develop their knowledge about and attitudes toward life. [1]

Those familiar with definitions of culture will notice that this definition gives strong emphasis to the process of symbolization, the consideration of system, and the role of shaping meaning. This is intentional, since the goal is to allow these considerations to interact closely with the more commonly explored historical and theological analyses of the relations between brothers and priests.

Before moving into the discussion proper, however, one more thing needs to be said. It must be remembered that this presentation on the relations between brothers and priests is from a cultural perspective, using the categories which have been developed in the discipline of cultural anthropology and sociology. Some of these categories will seem foreign to the theological perspective of the meaning and practice of religious life. It should be said at the outset that, although the study of culture is a study of one of the most pervasive aspects of the human environment, the categories of description and explanation used here are not intended to supersede or transcend theological ones. But they can provide perspectives which can help us think through again how we express evangelical and theological ideals, and may offer some suggestions for getting at problems that seem to be intractable for theological reflection.

The presentation here on cultural factors will be in three parts. The first part will look at the life of the religious institute within the culture of the Roman Catholic Church. The Church can be considered one of the cultures in which brothers and priests live, offering to them that system of symbols and inherited conceptions which Geertz defined as a culture. Certainly no comprehensive description of that culture can be given within the short compass of this presentation. A more restricted approach will be taken. We will look at the tension points between the religious institute and the larger Church. Points of tension often illuminate the respective symbolic configurations of the two parties better than separate descriptions of the two. We will look also at shifts going on in the religious institute and in the larger Church. Cultures are alive and not static; they constantly experience change. The life of the religious institute and of the Church as a whole is not different in that regard. It is hoped that by looking at the points of tension — in

both the creative and potentially destructive senses of that term —
we will come to some clearer understanding of the cultural issues
involved in brother-priest relations which impinge upon theological considerations.

The second part of this presentation will then turn to the
religious institute within the American cultural setting. By
"American" here is meant the dominant culture of the United
States. To be sure, religious institutes in the United States experience themselves as being part of more than the dominant, white,
male-directed culture in this country. Again, for a complete
cultural analysis, the full range of ethnic group, race, class and
gender would have to be taken into consideration. The reason for
concentrating on the dominant culture is that this culture has been
the major force to be reckoned with. It seems fair to say that most
male religious institutes have not yet come to terms with the
cultural transformations being wrought by feminist perspectives.
Likewise, the perspectives of racial and ethnic groups not fully
participating in that dominant culture still do not have the impact on
the values, ideals, symbols and meanings of a religious institute
which they deserve to have. As members of minority groups are
quick to point out, being excluded from the process of the dominant
culture does not mean that they do not have to deal with it. It is for
these reasons that the dominant culture will be given the prime
consideration here.

In the third section the results of the analyses of the first two
parts will be brought into conversation with each other. What can
an analysis of the relation between religious institutes and the larger
Church tell us about problems we might be able to resolve and
about creative tensions necessary for the health of both? In examining religious institutes within the dominant culture of the United
States, what can we learn about how cultural forces, both positive
and negative, both delimit and expand the range of our possibilities

in dealing with relations between brothers and priests? What impact might this have on our processes of formation, our spirituality, our mission?

Priest-Brother Relations in Ecclesiastical Culture

RELATIONS BETWEEN PRIESTS AND BROTHERS within religious institutes play themselves out at the boundary between two forms of social organization within the Church: an hierarchical and an egalitarian style of organization. Both of these kinds of organization have roots in the New Testament.

A hierarchical form of organization is characterized by an ordering of social roles toward an interrelated whole. In such an ordering, it is assumed that there is a division of labor — not everyone performs, or is capable of performing, the same function. The ordering can take place according to any number of principles, but it seems that almost always two factors come into play: power and status within the society being so ordered. Sometimes the factors of power and status coincide; in other instances they do not.[2]

In the case of the Church, both of these factors come into play. From an anthropological point of view, the hierarchical ordering is based on an access to sacred power, an access which in turn confers a certain status. The sacrament of Holy Orders can be seen as the boundary marker indicating entry to that realm of sacred power. Within that realm, there is of course a further ordering of access, with bishops representing the fullness of the Order, and priests and deacons participating in different fashions in that Order. The Pope stands at the apex of this ordering of access; although he may be technically seen only as a first among equals, the office carries with it a number of titles accumulated through the centuries. Perhaps the one most important for us here is that of ''Vicar of Christ''. In other words, no one has such immediate access to the Head of the Church as does the Pope.

Now this access to sacred power given by ordination marks a significant division in the body of the Church — the very use of the term "cleric" (from the Greek *kleros* — to be set apart) indicates that. A variety of boundary markers are set up to both maintain this division and in turn provide a source of identity for those in the clerical state. Celibacy is certainly principal among these. In many countries distinctive dress (sometimes for the lower clergy, almost always for the higher clergy) provides another marker.

It should be noted that while this was meant to insure a clear division of labor — only the clergy may provide access to divine power through the sacraments — the question of status and power is not so clear. The Catholic hierarchical ordering certainly is a sign of status, but it does not provide access to all the power. The status has been evident in special titles, privileges (immunity from civil prosecution, military service, and other civil responsibilities in many countries), but the matter of power is more ambiguous. While the routine access to divine power is the province of the clergy, there are other pathways which lie beyond clerical control: visions, healings, and the like can be found among any members of the Church.

Up until fairly recently, this form or ordering had held rather securely. It had been supported by two historical streams which had converged in the sixteenth century. One was a spirituality for priests based more on their sacred state than their spiritual service. It had grown up in the fifteenth century at a time of a surplus clergy; some justification had to be found for being a priest when the Christian community really had no need of so many. The name of Josse van Clichthove is connected with the development of this spirituality.[3]   The other was the Catholic Reform undertaken at the Council of Trent. This spirituality of state rather than function helped firm up the reform of the clergy which that Council intended. Together they became a powerful force for maintaining the hierarchical ordering of the Church.

However, there has always been a second movement along-side this hierarchical ordering, one more egalitarian in nature. The boundary of access to sacred power here is not drawn within the Church between those who have this power and those who do not; it is drawn around the whole Church, between those who are members and those who are not. Baptism, rather than Holy Orders, becomes the boundary marker for this access. In so doing, emphasis is laid on the fullness of participation in the life of Christ by each and every member of the Church.

Such an awareness is characteristic of an egalitarian ordering of society. Whereas the hierarchical ordering emphasizes the internal relations between the various members of a society, and how each contributes a portion to the whole, an egalitarian model emphasizes how each member embodies the whole. In such a model, role allocation remains more diffuse, and internal relations ambiguous or less defined. The equality and full participation of each member is the focus of attention. Boundary markers are set at the entry points to the community rather than at internal points in the community

The New Testament shows evidence of both of these impulses in early Christian communities. Perhaps the clearest contrast can be found co-existing within one part of the New Testament literature, the Pauline Corpus. Paul's discussion of the ordering of the gifts of the community along the analogy of the human body in I Corinthians 11 has often been called upon to support the hierarchical ordering of the Church. And the baptismal acclamation of Galatians 3:28 is the classic text supporting egalitarian models of the Christian community.

Religious institutes are perhaps the principal institutional heirs of this egalitarian strand of social organization.[4] Many have clear egalitarian impulses in their very founding, often even in conscious contrast to a more hierarchically ordered society. If one looks at how power and status function in these egalitarian societies, the chapter is usually the prime form of government, emphasizing that power lies ultimately in the whole body of members rather than ordained individuals. Status is often short-term, based on the will of the community (this has become increasingly the case). Compare this with how status and power are construed in a hierarchical ordering.

To be sure, the decision to permit members of the clergy to enter religious institutes in large numbers in the early history of the Church introduced the tension of hierarchical organization back into the heart of an egalitarian movement. It should also be noted that the role diffusion and ambiguously defined internal relations make egalitarian societies unstable over long periods of time, particularly when situations of conflict arise and in the transmittal of the egalitarian values to the next generation. Thus, many religious institutes went through a process in the second generation where their egalitarian style was accommodated (or, especially in the case of women's institutes, got accommodated) to the larger hierarchical ordering. And so the tensions of a hierarchical ordering (if the dark side of egalitarianism is instability, the dark side of hierarchy is social oppression) which the founding of a religious institute was intended to obviate find their way back into the very heart of the egalitarian creation.

Shifts in the Ecclesiastical Culture

TWO IMPORTANT SHIFTS are creating a redrawing of the boundary lines both within religious institutes and within the Church itself. From the perspective of the religious institutes, it is the call to return to the charism that shaped the founding of the institute. In this, members of institutes have been rediscovering those egalitarian roots. In some of the medieval orders, this has meant revaluing the fact that one is a member of the Order first and priest second. It has also led to an analysis of those elements added to the charism to accommodate it within a hierarchical ordering. Thus, brothers were clearly subordinated to priests in order to conform with the cleric-lay distinctions of a hierarchical ordering. And distinctive garb, reminiscent of the boundary markers of the clergy, was imposed as a way of aggregating the institute to the larger social organization of the Church.

This rediscovery of the egalitarian roots had led to a redefinition of constitutions, and in many instances, a replay of the tensions between egalitarian and hierarchical models that marked the founding of many institutes.

The second shift has affected the whole Church. The emphasis on baptism and the image of the Church as the People of God in *Lumen Gentium* enhanced the egalitarian model within the Church. By placing such emphasis on the boundary marker for entry into the Church (rather than internal boundary markers such as the Eucharist or Holy Orders), the conciliar texts opened the way for considerable egalitarian possibilities where once they had not been present. This was supported especially by rendering a more participative liturgy into the vernacular, and by opening liturgical functions to the non-clergy by means of postconciliar directives.

It is particularly the latter, the extension and acknowledgement of a broader range of ministries for all the members of the Church, that has created the greatest challenge for maintaining the hierarchical ordering of the Church. While hierarchy will not pass away (its roots are as ancient as the egalitarian ones), it will find itself undergoing considerable change, especially along its peripheries.

And it is along those peripheries that the tensions are most felt. The challenge (or the erosion, depending on one's perspective) is most keenly felt by those on that boundary: the priest and the deacon on the one side, those actively participating in the ministry of the Church as laypersons on the other. Lay ministers are doing more and more of what once were considered sacred acts reserved to the clergy. By assuming leadership within communities, they achieve not only status, but a considerable amount of the power attendant upon that status as well. Through education they exhibit an equal (and sometimes superior) competence to the clergy. Many clergy welcome this development, but in so doing cause some to question one of the factors that make hierarchies work: the social sanctions attendant upon hierarchy's division of labor. Put simply, the price of higher status in hierarchy is often restriction of certain social behaviors. Thus, as status in ministry becomes more and more ill-defined between lower clergy and laity, the clergy begin to question more vigorously restrictions on their social behavior: celibacy, restriction from elected political office and certain occupations, lifelong commitment, and so on. The restrictions are no longer being "rewarded," so to speak, by status.

In conclusion, then, by looking at the shifts taking place in ecclesiastical culture, we see both an internal factor — the renewal of religious life — and an external factor — the resurgence of an officially sanctioned egalitarian model within a hierarchically defined Church — combining to create a powerful stimulus for rethinking roles within religious institutes. To complete the picture for U.S. religious institutes, we need to engage in a similar analysis of the dominant culture in this country.

Social Relations in U.S. Culture

THE FOUNDING of the American Republic was seen by many as an experiment in a new form of social organization. This form would embody a principle which had been taking shape in European Enlightenment thinking, namely, a principle focusing upon the individual and the individual's essential equality and dignity among other individuals. The thrust of this development carried with it a certain antihierarchical strain. In hierarchies, the individual has dignity and rights, but always understood within an ordered whole. Thus each individual within the hierarchy does not enjoy the same rights or the same dignity; each is ordered into an assigned place within the whole. In the egalitarian form of thinking, the individual is not part of the whole; rather, the whole (the full dignity of what it means to be human) is present, at least potentially, in each individual. Whereas status and state are key concepts for hierarchy, equality became the key concept in this new form of social organization.

In the dominant culture which was to take shape in the United States this sense of equality was yoked with individualism, a not unlikely partner. Early observers, such as Alexis de Toqueville in the 1830's, were keenly interested as to whether equality and individualism could give direction to a society, whether the yoked pair might not always be pulling in different directions. There has clearly been a tension throughout U.S. history in this regard, and many of the questions about what holds the policy together continue to plague Americans.[5]

Our task here is to identify some of those cultural characteristics which cluster around egalitarianism and individualism and see how they have influenced religious life in the U.S., especially in priest-brother relations. It should be noted at the outset that these characteristics will be described in terms of the cultural ideals rather than their somewhat more checkered actual performance. For while Americans profess equality and look at themselves as an egalitarian society, a great number of formal hierarchies exist: in the corporate workplace, in the armed services, in healthcare systems. Moreover, American society is not as classless as it would want to consider itself, and ugly wounds of racial division mar its contours as well. These must always be borne in mind in such a discussion.

One consequence of a doctrine of equality is that status will be by and large achieved by individuals rather than ascribed to them. Ascribed status will generally be considered inferior to achieved status. This grows out of the doctrine that all are created equal, at least in potentiality. Status ascribed is something coming from the outside, and therefore not intrinsic.

Thus when brothers perform the same work as priests, and achieve the same level of education, the ascribed status of ordination ceases to carry much weight. In institutes where the previous divisions of labor and education are maintained, the ascribed status can be read as achievement (particularly in the matter of education). The American myth of achievement tends to be far stronger than any traditional theology of ordination and priesthood for many.

A second consequence of a culture of equality is that to maintain relationships between equals, all relationships tend to become more or less equal. Were that not the case, rankings among individuals would quickly set in. In point of fact, experience shows that it is impossible to maintain this ideal: some people become more emotionally important to us than others; some people we wish to meet only within certain spheres (such as the workplace); others take on superior rank for us by dint of their achievements; and others exercise coercive power over us. Americans hold on to their cultural ideal by introducing a number of accommodations:[6] studied informality, introduction of ambiguity in all relationships, and compartmentalization.

In studied informality, Americans go quickly to calling people, including people they barely know, by their first names. This will be used even in clearly non-egalitarian situations, as when an employer calls in an employee to deliver the pink slip of termination. Foreigners find this practice of using first names puzzling. At first it seems refreshing to some, but it obscures the status of relationships, and makes it difficult for foreigners to know how to position themselves. The studied informality also sometimes requires inquiring about intimate personal or family details even though there is no commitment to extending one's relationship in that direction.

The ambiguity in all relationships is a consequence of this studied informality. By maintaining a certain egalitarian ideal it becomes extremely difficult to estimate when a relationship is more than casual. Americans rarely use the word "acquaintance"; everyone is a "friend." This had led many foreigners to perceive Americans as being quite superficial in all their relationships. What this cultural peculiarity allows Americans to do is to acknowledge the full dignity of each of their acquaintances by assigning them the status of friend, but it often seems to inhibit genuine friendship as understood in many other cultures.

What keeps these egalitarian relationships together then? As many foreigners have noted, many of those relationships are not maintained. As Americans move, they often change friends and have little recourse to previous circles of acquaintances. Compartmentalization — friends at work, in the neighborhood, in voluntary organizations — provides another way of maintaining networks of relations relatively independent of one another.

Now this may all sound somewhat negative about how the egalitarian ethos functions within American society. Americans, after all, are capable of having close relations with other people. But in order for a society to function as well as American society has been able to do, it needs to bring egalitarian ideals in line with other exigencies. These three factors allow the egalitarian ideal to function at least as an ideal alongside the inequalities of society. Perhaps as importantly, they make the individualism of American society — also part of the cultural ideal — a possible part of this total configuration.

It is possible to have an egalitarian ideal of society without an individualist ideal. Most utopian (and religious) communities have been founded along those lines. Individuals within those communities experience a sense of equality and participation, but all submit themselves to the good of the entire community, either through the agency of common decision-making or some common rule. American society was unique in trying to combine egalitarianism with individualism on a large scale in the eighteenth century.

What might be considered the characteristics of individualism, especially as found in an egalitarian society?[7] Among those which could be listed are the inviolability of the individual (often defined in terms of rights), ambiguity about authority, commitment to pluralism as an ideal, and a lack of tradition as orienting the present and future.

In a situation of individualism, the individual is considered the basic unit of society, not the family, the clan or the society itself. Discussion of rights begins and ends with the individual. When this is coupled with egalitarianism, societies can tend toward a certain atomistic quality unless other factors come into play. America's extensive economic opportunity and sense of endless frontier provided a forum that allowed the individualism of much of the population to move as it would. In other words, if the resources for the expression of individual preference are available in sufficient amount, there is no need to raise questions about what might be holding things together.

How authority and power are exercised becomes an ambiguous thing in an individualist egalitarian society, mainly because it becomes difficult to locate the source of authority. In such instances, while authority is often far more constrained in terms of potentially oppressive measures, its diffusion may mean that it is reduced to power — who can seize the resources and impose their will.

In an individualist egalitarian society, pluralism is not an option; it becomes a necessity and an ideal. For it is only via a pluralism that a co-existence among differing sets of values and ideas can be achieved and maintained.

Finally, tradition does not provide a reliable guide in an individualist egalitarian society as it looks to its present and to its future. Tradition has a hard time accounting for the shifting perspectives and new configurations of individuals. The sense of direction must remain with the individuals.

Shifts Within U.S. Religious Life

THE SHIFT toward a greater sense of egalitarianism after the Second Vatican Council coincided with a shift in American Catholic life that had been taking shape since the 1950's. After living with an European immigrant consciousness since the 1830's, American Catholics found themselves entering the mainstream of American culture in the 1960's. By the mid-1970's, Roman Catholics were not only the largest Christian communion in the United States, they also had the highest median educational and income level — and this despite a still large immigrant segment in their ranks.

The renewal of religious life coincided then with this other cultural force. Heretofore the internal relational patterns of most religious institutes mirrored rather well those of their European counterparts. Patterns of hierarchy within American religious institutes would not have been that different from anywhere else in the world. In matters of internal relations, at least, American religious institutes were a countervailing if not countercultural sign within their American environment. A spirituality of world renunciation only reinforced this.

The Vatican II call for the renewal of religious life was magnified in the American context by the Church's entry into the mainstream of the culture. Such an entry implied at least some acceptance of the cultural ideals of that context. It would be my contention that American religious institutes have accepted the cultural ideals of individualist egalitarianism to a great extent in the matter of their social organization. In this regard they are not a countervailing force in the culture as they had often been in the Church. They are surely more authentically American in this regard. To be sure, commitments to social justice are in far greater evidence in the 1980's than they were in the 1950's; although even here justice is sometimes defined in terms of individualist egalitarianism as undifferentiated equality.[8]

As one examines the internal relations in religious institutes of men today, the hierarchical style is often still very much in evidence, though assuredly less so than was the case two decades previously. Internal relations reinforce this diminution of clerical-lay divide: rules are cast in more general form, thus introducing more ambiguity in social relations; divisions of labor are not as sharply defined; divisions in allocations of space have often been abolished; financial positions have been equalized. Brothers no longer see themselves as servants of the priests and mere support staff; priests are unsure exactly what the brothers' role is. Decision-making is much more on a shared basis.

Nearly everyone would say that all these things are benefits gained from reducing and trying to eliminate the clerical-lay divide. In agreeing with this, one finds oneself in step with a progressive movement within the Church and with the ideals of the dominant culture. But all cultural ideals have their challenge and their dark sides as well. It is now time to turn to the challenges and tensions to ask questions about the future.

The Future of Brother-Priest Relations: Challenges and Tensions

GIVEN THIS ANALYSIS of ecclesiastical and national culture, what challenges does the U.S. dominant culture offer to religious institutes, both as ways of enchancing our mission and as potentially blind spots to be monitored? Within the short scope of this chapter, based as it is on quite summary analyses of Church and culture, challenges can be presented only by way of questions and suggestions. That we are most clearly situated in an ecclesiastical as well as a national culture is evident from the experience of many American provinces with the missions they have established outside this country. Different configurations of relations between brothers and priests confront the patterns of the home province. In some countries (such as in Latin America) where evangelization has become the ministry priority, brothers are better equipped to carry out the ministry than priests who are confined by traditional sacramental roles. The experience of solidarity comes, too, as a challenge to the individualism of U.S. culture. In yet other places, a failure to appreciate the dynamics of a hierarchical civil society makes a more egalitarian style simply not understood rather than countercultural.

A first consequence of this analysis is to realize the large amount of compatibility between the American individualist-egalitarian ideal and the more egalitarian movement growing out of the Second Vatican Council. The American experience provides important resources for the new relationships between hierarchical and egalitarian movements in the Church. The experience of Americans with democracy adds an important element heretofore largely lacking in ecclesiastical experience. As a corollary to this, American religious should be especially attentive to those areas of American life where the egalitarian ideal is not lived out: the instances of racism, classism and sexism.

Secondly, within the confines of a religious institute's internal relations, a model might be able to be developed to help deal with the new identities needed for both clergy and laity, based on the experience of new relations between clergy and laity within institutes, and the attempts of many institutes to introduce some kind of associate membership. Of course, some of the nagging problems of the larger clergy-lay problem will not be alleviated in this (e.g., in a religious institute both brothers and priests are celibate, whereas this would not be the case in the larger Church problem); but the attempt to find an overarching vision for both brothers and priests (this often being done in the process of developing a mission statement for the province or institute) can offer a paradigm for resolving identity crises of both clergy and laity in the larger Church.

At the same time, religious institutes should be aware that their population makes up only a small part of the total Church. Consequently, they will continue to feel the pressures of the clergy-lay distinction even when they feel that they have come to some reasonable solution themselves. There is a temptation to try to live in splendid isolation, a temptation that offers only illusions rather than resolutions.

A third consideration focuses especially on the individualism to which American religious are heir. The clerical-lay divide can appear to be overcome because of the individualism within an institute. Thus there is such ambiguity in all the relations that issues of social groups barely emerge. In such instances one must ask hard questions about the quality of relations. This is especially important in a highly individualist society which is inevitably somewhat antithetical to a sense of community. "Community" has taken on some of the vague meaning in American culture as has "friend." Robert Bellah has suggested that what most Americans call community might better be called "lifestyle enclave."[9]   This means that people are drawn together by common patterns of living rather than any deeply shared values. Does this happen in some of our institutes, where we agree to disagree, seek only "support" (often a name for one of those ambiguous social relationships) from other members as our prime mode of relationship?

This leads to a fourth consideration. Accepting the model of individualist egalitarianism means also confronting its dark side. As a form of social organization it works best in situations of relative prosperity where each may pursue a separate path. But if one starts speaking of solidarity, of options for the poor — those without such resources — to what extent does the cultural ideal remain an ideal for the religious institute? There have been rather grotesque instances where they have combined, as in situations where religious engage in a kind of tourism to show their solidarity with the poor, with refugees, with the imprisoned. While it fulfills personal ideals, does it really engage the mission of the institute as it might?

Fifth, in trying to overcome some of the problems of the clerical-lay divide, might not the analysis include comparing the relative advantages and disadvantages of individualist and utopian egalitarianism? Many religious institutes were founded under the guidance of a kind of utopian egalitarianism, but often it was already too infected with non-egalitarian forms. The legacy of clericalism with which we now struggle is a significant part of that. But might not a reconsideration of utopian egalitarianism — a vision of what society might be like and what an institute's mission is within that vision — provide an alternative for what can become the atomism of the cultural ideal?

Sixth, the considerable concern with formation and the definition of mission now part of the consciousness of religious institutes is indicative of the reflection already going on around these matters. It seems important not to allow an ethnocentrism to creep into all of this, whereby ideals of the dominant culture are canonized. Listening to the voices of minorities in this country, and the experiences of members working in other countries, can help American religious question in a constructive fashion some of their own presuppositions. Trying to subject the social organization of the dominant culture to an analysis usually reserved for other peoples' cultures is a way to help create such a healthy self-awareness.

Conclusion

THE TENSION between hierarchical and egalitarian models of social organization within the Church is an ancient one, and one that will not go away. At its best, the tension holds together two sets of ideals — one of showing forth the cooperation and unity among believers with one stressing the dignity and full participation of all believers. At their worst the one becomes oppressive to those on the bottom and the other ignores the rest in a kind of egotism. The American context for religious life offers, from a cultural perspective, both constructive prospects and potentially destructive tendencies. It is in a continued and carefully shared attempt at exploring new models that we can hope to make headway in the common mission of Jesus Christ.

Endnotes

1 Clifford Geertz, *The Interpretation of Cultures* New York: Basic Books, 1973, p. 89.

2 Still the most comprehensive discussion of power and status as they affect hierarchy can be found in Louis Dumont, *Homo Hierarchicus: The Caste System and Its Implications* Chicago: The University of Chicago Press, 1970.

3 See the discussion of this spirituality in Edward Schillebeeckx, *Ministry* New York: Crossroad, 1981, pp. 58-65.

4 Other heirs would be lay associations which did not become religious institutes, such as the Beguines and the groups associated with shrines and feasts.

5 This is best articulated in Robert Bellah et al., *Habits of the Heart: Individualism and Commitment in American Life* Berkeley: the University of California Press, 1985. The subtitle of the book sums up the concern of the authors.

6 The most acute analysis of American social patterns I have found in Edward C. Stewart, *American Culture Patterns: A Cross-Culture Perspective* Chicago: Intercultural Press, 1972. I owe much to his analysis in my presentation here.

7 Examples of such societies where individualism is prized yet are not strictly egaliterian would be nomadic societies living by herding or hunting.

8 Cf. especially Dumont, op. cit., especially the Introduction and Chapter 8.

9 Bellah, op. cit., pp. 71-75.

Theological Explorations in Service of a Pastoral Imperative

THOMAS E. CLARKE, S.J.

A T THE OUTSET let me say that this essay will not meet the expectations of readers who are looking for *a theology* of the place of brothers in clerical religious communities. My intent here is not theology but to theologize. Though it is generally convenient to use a substantive — theology — to designate what is primarily an exercise of reflective faith, our times have brought a renewed accent on theologizing as a constitutive element in the social praxis of the gospel. My goal here is to evoke and inform, by my theologizing, the active exercise of theologizing on the part of each reader.

Second, there are many ways of theologizing, and today we can distinguish three major ones: *magisterial*, the theologizing of bishops and their associates in the important role of safeguarding and handing on the deposit of the faith; *academic* (or *professional*), the kind that seeks to advance the frontiers of understanding within the context of new cultural influences and needs; and a new way, commonly called *theological reflection*, which I shall describe more in detail, as it is the way which I shall be following here.

As I have elsewhere described, this new way of theologizing differs notably from the other two ways in several respects: its *ecclesial location* is the "grassroots" of the Church in some real sense; its *primary agent* is a reflective *community* of Christians; its *immediate goal* is the transformation through decision and action of some aspect of human life; and its *method* may be briefly identified as *praxis*.[1]   The specific method followed and adapted here is familiar to many CMSM members, the so called "pastoral circle" developed by the Center of Concern, which seems to be finding increasing use. This way and this specific method differ notably from the academic and magisterial ways in several respects: it is more integrative and holistic; it draws more immediately on the revelatory experience of the theologizing community; its utilization of the secular social sciences is conducted within a Christian social analysis; and it is more directly ordered to discerning decision and responsive action.

What I propose to do in this essay, then, is to illustrate by practice how the reality of the life of religious brothers within clerical communities can be material for theologizing on the part of communities and groups which desire to bring the transforming power of the Gospel to bear on this stressful and not fully redeemed ecclesial situation. By outlining this way of theologizing, I hope that others, especially in groups, will profitably engage in similar exercises. The four sections of the essay are illustrative of the four phases of the pastoral circle. From the start I would insist that each of these several behaviors is an instance of theologizing. This is true even though they differ widely from one another, and we are not yet accustomed to considering some of them, particularly the sharing revelatory experience, as more than a prelude or appendage to "real theology."

1. Experience

ACADEMIC AND MAGISTERIAL WAYS in theology tend to consider the Christian experience of the theologizer irrelevant, or at least merely dispositive for the task of theologizing. Theological reflection, on the contrary, *requires* that the personal and communal story, as carrier of revelatory experience, be included, even perhaps as the starting point of the total process. Ideally, I would be doing this now within some group, though it can also be done through the medium of writing, as I am now doing.

My Jesuit life began in 1941 at St. Andrew-on-Hudson, our novitiate just north of Poughkeepsie. I occasionally return there, though it is now a prestigious cooking school, to visit the graves of Pierre Teilhard de Chardin and other Jesuits buried there beside the Hudson. The following scenario would also apply to later years of study, in the middle and late 1940's, within a community of almost three hundred Jesuits, at Woodstock College in the Maryland countryside west of Baltimore. In both places our life was considerably more monastic than Ignatius had in mind for his "contemplatives in action," even during their years of preparation for ministry. Silence outside the times of formal recreation, the wearing of habits and sometimes birettas, meals taken usually in silence while listening to some edifying reading — these were a few of the important symbolic structures. More relevant to the present theme, our life in this "total institution" was divided into three overlapping subcultures — Fathers, scholastics, and brothers. Each group had its own recreation room, and sat together in the refectory. The brothers, of course, wore no biretta (in the sixteenth and seventeenth centuries this had been a live issue) and no linen or plastic collar with their habits. They were for the most part engaged in domestic tasks, in kitchen, clothes room, supply room, boiler room, garden, and the like. Each morning there was a "brothers' Mass," celebrated at six o'clock. In those days vocations to the Jesuit brotherhood were still fairly numerous, and so at St.

Andrew's and Woodstock the brothers formed a sizable group (ranging from fifteen to twenty) within the larger community.

It is more difficult to convey my experience of the relationships which lay beneath the numbers and the formal structures. I shared with my fellow scholastics — and later at Woodstock with my fellow faculty members — a feeling for the brothers that was positive, warm, reverent, somewhat sentimental, and in retrospect subtly elitist. Then, as now, I viewed Jesuit brothers as the real contemplatives of our Society, and considered many of the brothers to be really holy, as indeed they were. They seemed to me to fulfill simultaneously the roles of Martha and Mary. All of us had been given, from novitiate days on, the image of St. Alphonsus Rodriguez as the quintessential Jesuit brother, celebrated by our own Gerard Manley Hopkins: "those years and years of world without event/That in Majorca Alfonso watched the door."[2]   We assumed that, with rare exception, Jesuit brothers were called to be consecrated domestics, providing the basic conditions for Jesuit priests and scholastics to engage in the apostolate. Our Jesuit Institute seemed to support this understanding, especially since we knew little or nothing of the history of the brothers within our Society. We took special comfort in the fact that a brother, René Goupil, was the first of the Jesuit martyrs of North America, and we were vaguely aware of a few famous brothers, such as Andrea Pozzo, whose frescoes still adorn the church of St. Ignatius and other churches in Rome. When the brothers at Woodstock celebrated the feast of St. Ignatius at a meal served by the scholastics, or when all the brothers of the province assembled once a year for a special celebration, the rest of us felt a warm family glow, grateful that they were part of our life.

Still under the surface of these conscious feelings what was going on in the brothers themselves and in the rest of us? It was impossible at that time to say, since the culture of our common life did not provide a forum for the sharing of inner feelings, angers, frustrations. To suggest that the later language of societal sin or institutional violence might be applied to the culture of St. Andrew's or Woodstock would have shocked and perhaps scandalized most of us. But then, this passive acceptance of the given was an attitude which extended to the whole of our life together during those decades prior to the period when the winds of change, troubling and refreshing, began to blow.

Two events, one in 1969, the other in 1974-75, form important milestones for my personal experience of the changes of attitudes and structures which were to take place regarding Jesuit brothers. In August of 1969, a twelve-day conference of a hundred and thirty Jesuit brothers and priests at the University of Santa Clara recommended significant changes in both outlook and arrangements. Much of the language was blandly inspirational, but there were several innovative suggestions, including

> the desirability of an eventual updating of the canonical status of the Society of Jesus from that of an order of clerks regular to a classification that would recognize it as a community of Ignatian, apostolic religious, lay and clerical . . . the desirability of an extensive and even radical change regarding active and passive voice for all Jesuits, brothers and priests, in the government of the Society . . . the desirability of having the form of final profession the same for all. . .[3]

Such recommendations, which reflected a passionate movement in the middle and late sixties among a small but determined group of U.S. Jesuits, were too radical to carry the day. The Santa Clara conference had been held in preparation for a world congress of Jesuit brothers in Rome in 1970. Neither that congress, nor the 32nd General Congregation in 1974-75, chose to speak of the Society of Jesus as being primarily an apostolic community of priest and brothers. Under the watchful eye of the Holy See, both gatherings elected to abide by the traditional conception of the Society of Jesus as a clerical institute, a sacerdotal community governed by priests. A strong inclination on the part of the 32nd General Congregation, following widespread sentiment throughout our society, to extend the profession of four solemn vows to all Jesuits, whether priests or brothers, was abruptly terminated by Paul VI himself, who saw in this move a dangerous downplaying of the sacerdotal character of the Society, and a weakening of the intimate bond uniting it to the Pope. The Vatican's displeasure with widespread dissent and criticism of Rome on the part of Jesuits in the Vatican II era became interwoven with its refusal of this structural change within the Order so closely associated with it.[4]

For me this history was both saddening and clarifying. Strongly believing that the empowerment of the laity is a key sign of our times, increasingly drawn for both theological and pastoral reasons to relativize the weight of priestly ordination in comparison with the import of baptismal and religious vows, and attracted by the image of the Society of Jesus as an apostolic collaboration of lay and clerical Christians, I was inclined to feel that we had missed an opportunity for creative development of our charism. At the same time I was brought to see that the Society of Jesus, under some duress, had chosen to continue to identify itself as a sacerdotal community, notwithstanding that a significant portion of its membership was not called to sacerdotal office, and notwithstanding that great numbers of its ordained priests were engaged primarily in ministries which did not require Church office for their exercise. Given this choice of identity, I can appreciate the congruity of governmental authority continuing to remain with ordained priests. As for the exclusion of Jesuit brothers from the four solemn vows, it is a *fait accompli*, at least for the present. In my opinion its import is greatly reduced by the fact that the distinction of solemn and simple vows, together with the special vow of obedience to the Pope taken by some Jesuits, has become for the most part a ritual irrelevancy, so far as the lives of individual Jesuits are concerned.

Despite this decision to continue with our traditional formal structure, the actual living situations of our society today strongly contrast with those of St. Andrew's and Woodstock. For almost all of us, the religious habit has disappeared, and the biretta lives only in comic memory. The era of separate tables and separate recreation rooms is gone. There are far fewer brothers, of course (less than four hundred in the United States, about fifty in my own New York Province). Without an unexpected reversal of trends in vocations, they may all but disappear from our membership by the turn of the century.

Of greater significance is the development of the training, skills, and roles of Jesuit brothers during the past few decades. A sprinkling of them serve within local communities in the role of *minister*, that is, the one who, while not strictly a superior, directs and coordinates the practical and material side of community life. Apostolically, a good many brothers have moved into ministries previously reserved to priests and scholastics. For example Brother Jim Kenny, a pioneer in developing interest and change regarding the vocation of the Jesuit brother, had before his death in 1985 become vice-president and treasurer of Fordham University. Brother Rich Curry, chairman of the National Jesuit Brothers' Committee, is director of the National Theatre Workshop of the Handicapped. Despite such breakthroughs, however, the image of the Jesuit brother as a consecrated domestic lingers among the general public, and perhaps among a good number of Jesuits.

These several paragraphs have been a small sample of the first phase of the pastoral circle, and they lead me to ask: at the end of this reminiscence, how do I find myself? What feelings do I experience, and how would I image these feelings? Questions such as these, though irrelevant for other ways in theology, are integral to the endeavor of theological reflection. Responding to them, even in fragmentary fashion, can help bring important energies to the subsequent tasks of analysis, reflection, and decision. This is especially true when the stories and attendant feelings and images are shared within a group. The resulting sympathy and sense of solidarity can provide such a group with a momentum and stamina enabling it to weather subsequent tensions.

In the present case I would say that I feel chagrined at much that I have experienced of the history of the Jesuit brothers during the past few decades. I am distressed at what I perceive as a missed opportunity for my community to accommodate its charism, its structures, and its attitudes more fully to that sign of the times which is the empowerment of the laity. At the same time I am resigned to taking as a given, at least for a few decades, the prevailing self-image of the Society of Jesus as a sacerdotal community. I am heartened by the fact that such a self-image has not totally blocked the gradual change of relationships between Jesuit brothers and other Jesuits, both within our various ministries and in our domestic life.

The image which occurs to me as congruous with all this is that of a rich family whose yacht has run aground on a desert island. On the high seas, as back at the manor house, family members related to the servants and crew in more or less of an "Upstairs/ Downstairs" fashion. Prescribed rituals touching dress, forms of address, and other behaviors judged appropriate or not for each group, effected two highly differentiated subcultures within a general culture. But after a few months on the desert island, the exigencies of survival have brought a very different kind of world, where there are no separate tables, no distinctive dress, and no sharp distinctions in the way that individuals relate to one another. The drastically changed situation of this group of human beings has produced remarkable changes touching vision and values, the exercise of power, and the common daily expressions of respect and regard for one another. This is not to say that there is never any instinctive regression to the former situation. Still, something definitive has happened in the life of the group. Such a change, basically cultural in character though facilitated by juridical and theological changes, has taken place in the Society of Jesus during the past three or four decades. On balance, it has been a salutary change.

II. Social Analysis

A SECOND KIND OF THEOLOGICAL EXERCISE within the total process seeks an analytical understanding of the situation of brothers within religious (here Jesuit) communities. A first step is to gather the empirical data needed for sound analysis. Here is where a reflecting group can facilitate its task by drawing on existing studies done by specialists. Though no one has written a comprehensive history of the vocation of the Jesuit brother, an excellent long essay by George Ganss provided abundant background, stretching from the emergence of that vocation in Ignatius' own lifetime to the most recent history.[5] A few examples of such relevant data must suffice for present purposes. In the sea of change that took place over the past several decades, what were the differences in the background of candidates for admission as brothers, differences touching social and economic status, ethnic origin, degree and kind of formal education, age, experience of the professional or business scene, practice of prayer and devotion, and the like? Another example: At what point did the laws or customs of the Society of Jesus assign separate tables and recreation rooms to priests, scholastics, and brothers, and what lay behind such prescriptions? I like to place this empirical (in contrast to the experiential) element at the beginning of the second phase of the process, because it is integral to the analytical treatment of what has been experienced, and because it shares in the detached, objective character of analysis.

Complete social and cultural analysis of an ecclesial situation serves as an horizon always in view but never fully attained. One must be content to do what one can with the resources at hand.

Even when a group draws on the skills of professional analysis, there will always be something left out or something obscure. In the present case, I will offer just a few examples of how social analysis can enlighten a study of change in the status of brothers in clerical communities.

A first perspective is to look at the structuring of life in the period prior to change and then in the period after change. How structured was life in each phase? What were the significant structures in which common meanings and values found expression? What were those meanings and values? To ask such questions is to place the question of culture and inculturation, a question which touches more deeply on life than questions of an economic or political kind, though these also have their place.

Let us take, for example, in the story I have sketched, the structure of separate tables and separate recreation rooms in the period prior to change, and the disappearance of such structures in the course of change. What was the community in effect saying when, in earlier centuries of our Society's history, it established such arrangements? A careful historical analysis might disclose considerable complexity. Did such a choice reflect the class consciousness of the surrounding European society and, more broadly, a lingering of the medieval view that each entity in the universe has its natural place? To what extent was it inspired by Ignatius' personal insistence on right order as indispensable for the apostolic efficacy of his company? Or, on the contrary, did it represent, at some stressful or confused moment of our history, a dissonance with earlier practice, and perhaps a defensive absolutizing of what till then had been treated as something relative? Could it be that, while it may have been legitimate, even necessary, in the period of its institution, it had become through the subtle vicissitudes of history a frozen symbol which no one had the courage or imagination to change until the Vatican II period?

Similarly, a group engaged in social analysis of such structures would look for the meaning and values contained in the initiatives for change, and in the alternative structures, or lack thereof, which replaced the traditional ones. Here too a great deal of complexity may attend the analysis. The general restlessness and questioning of tradition and authority characteristic of the 1960s would certainly be a factor. The return of Roman Catholicism to a direct seeking of vitality from the Scriptures and the early Church probably helped to intensify a growing repugnance with this ritual separation of Christian brothers living in the same apostolic community. In the United States the influence of the egalitarianism of our history was undoubtedly a factor, though its comparative weight might need to be sorted out by examining the extent to which Jesuits in Europe and elsewhere were feeling the same impatience with structures now judged to be divisive. And the contagious spirit of Vatican II was surely being felt within our communities. The decree on religious life, for example, called for sweeping revision in which "constitutions, directories, custom books, books of prayer and ceremonies, and similar compilations are to be suitably revised. . . This task will call for the suppression of outmoded regulations."[6]

It is clear, then, that an important part of social analysis of the change we have experiencd will be to look at the structural aspect of the situations prior to and consequent upon change, and to state what we perceive to be the important factors helping to constitute such situations.

A second perspective is to analyze the contrasting situations from the standpoint of power and energy. Here is where the common practice of political analysis can be broadened and deepened and adapted in a Christian social analysis. In this regard the distinction of formal and informal power is important. In traditional, heirarchically ordered societies such as the Society of Jesus, the sharpness of the contrast between the powerful and the powerless is often offset by the presence of considerable informal power. How many major superiors in the early months of their government experience this fact of life in a melancholy way! In analysis one needs to go beyond the power immediately connected with decision-making, and touch on other potencies which release another kind of energy into the life of a community. Think, for example, of the potency of a helpless newborn infant within a family. Social analysis of the situation at St. Andrew's or Woodstock in the 1940s will disclose that the score or more of brothers, though virtually deprived of important decision-making power, exercised great potency in shaping the life of the community. Especially at the period when, in the early 1960s, many scholastics and some faculty members were passionate for change, for example through the opening of our refectory to women guests, a half conscious anxiety about how this might affect the brothers was an important factor in the exercise of power. Needless to say, this informal power was not monolithic among the brothers themselves; because of differences in age, educational background, and personal history, they took different attitudes towards the opening up of our common life during this period. Nevertheless, as the sub-group which our Jesuit culture had for centuries viewed as consecrated domestics akin to the oblates of the monastic tradition, our brothers had the most to lose in the breaking down of a kind of Jesuit monasticism. In addition, since they had less access to the theological and pastoral influences which were spurring such changes, they were being asked to endorse, or at least acquiesce to, rather drastic changes in life style which called into question some of their most cherished assumptions.

These are just a few of the perspectives which can be taken in the course of social analysis. A group engaged in this activity will find help with respect to the content of analysis in several of the other essays in this volume, particularly those dealing with history, culture, and psychology, and with respect to the process of analysis in some of the schemas offered to facilitate the practice of the pastoral circle.

Two further remarks may be helpful before moving on to the third phase of the process. First, by actual practice each group will find its way between what I would call "expertism," that is, a self-depreciating reliance on analysis done by specialists independently of a faith perspective, and, on the other hand, a narrow inability to transcend the limitations of personal experience and subjective attitudes of the members of the group. Such a balance is, of course, easier to describe than to achieve.

Second, I would highlight again the importance of culture as the deepest level of power shaping community life, and as underlying other important forms of power. More specifically, we can be helped if we regard the charism of our community as necessarily inculturated in specific and changing ways. In recent years I have come to see that there is such a thing as Jesuit culture, or rather a multiplicity of Jesuit cultures, each of which embodies the Ignatian myth and vision within a complexus of cultural forms. These forms are in constant need of analysis, in a view of the evaluation and revision which we now proceed to describe.

III. Theological Reflection

THE THIRD PHASE of the pastoral circle is designated as theological reflection, understood in a more restricted sense than in the title of the total process. It can be broadly divided into two phases, *evaluation* and *revision* (in the sense of re-envisioning, as shall be explained). In the first of these two exercises we take the experienced and analyzed situation and expose it to the light of the Gospel, the ultimate objective criterion in any discernment process. Making use of the Scriptures, of Church teaching, of the normative expression of our charism in Constitutions and similar enactments, and also of a sound theological statement on religious life and its meaning and value within the Church and in human society, this evaluative phase of the process seeks to identify and name what is sinful and what is graced in the situation under scrutiny.

It seems obvious that the complexity attending the analysis of the concrete situation of brothers within clerical communities is, if anything, intensified when the process moves on to evaluating structures and attitudes by the light of the Gospel. Two opposite hazards must be successfully handled. The first is the tendency to absolutize what is basically contingent in human relationships, for example to demand absolutely or to reject out of hand full equality in active and passive voice for priests and brothers within any religious community, regardless of charism, history, and contemporary circumstances. A similar absolutizing would consist in invoking one Gospel saying of Jesus or one statement of the charismatic founder and making it an immutable principle not subject to the processes of history and hermeneutics. The opposite hazard is to approach the present call of the community, along with the structural consequences of such a call, as if the community were being founded in the twentieth century, with no significant journey in history to assist in guiding present choices. Whatever the hazards, we need to make Christian choices and are capable of making them. An orderly process can facilitate such choices, and evaluating our present situation is an important phase of such a process.

As material for illustrating this phase of the pastoral circle it would be possible to choose a concrete feature of the present situation such as the fact that, within the Jesuit community, the office of superior is reserved to priests. The thrust of this reflection would bring to bear on this important structure — which dates from our origins — what is new in our experience of ecclesial and Jesuit life. Does this particular structure foster or impede the fulfillment of our apostolic mission? The question appears simple, but responding to it involves disentangling several interwoven threads of charism and history: the persevering conviction of our sacerdotal character as a community; the special role of the manifestation of conscience in the relation of each Jesuit with his superior; the sea change that has taken place in our realization of the baptismal call to holiness and apostolate; and so forth. Eventually such an evaluation would yield a common conviction regarding the value of the structure in question.

I prefer to develop more fully, however, an aspect of the present situation which is less tangible but more important than the one just described. I refer to the prevailing cultural and theological attitudes among Jesuits towards the comparative importance of baptismal vows, religious vows and priestly ordination. This matter has even greater subtlety and complexity than the question of the office of superior. Here I can offer a sketch of how it might be dealt with by a group in the evaluative phase of the circle.

First, evaluating this specific mindset supposes that it has been dealt with in the two preceding phases of the circle, hence that we have shared our story regarding it and that we have dealt with it through some social analysis. The remarks which follow will, for the sake of both brevity and comprehension, fuse the experiential, analytical and evaluative treatment of this topic, a procedure which is not generally to be recommended in group work.

At the time of my ordination to the priesthood in 1950, I understood the sacramental "character" of baptism, confirmation, and orders as producing within the recipient an ontological change of some kind, and I understood this to be more or less Church dogma. Such a view made it logical for me to formulate the distinction between the priesthood of all the baptized and ordained priesthood as an essential distinction. In addition, though I had known it from reading St. Francis de Sales that all Christians are called to holiness, the fact that baptism is a matter of vowing was lost on me, so that I understood the vowed life as religious life.

Subsequent reading and reflection during the fifties and sixties led me to abandon such views. Ordination came to have less an ontological than a social and functional significance, and religious vows were seen as specifications of baptismal vows. In trying to understand my own Jesuit priesthood and that of my Jesuit brothers, I passed through several phases where, for example,

I was attracted to the language of "the hyphenated priest," a term originating in the experience of many Jesuits who exercised priestly orders only within a larger ministry which they shared with others who were not priests. The priest-scientist, especially in the commanding figure of Pierre Teilhard de Chardin, was seen by me and others as perhaps the most characteristic version of a peculiarly Jesuit call. Eventually, however, I found such a view inadequate, and arrived at my present understanding. Because it touches on the place of brothers in our Society, I sketch it out here as an element of theological reflection.

First, baptismal vows are the most basic orientation of Christian faith, to which both religious vows and priestly ordination must look for their energy sources, and compared to which the latter two forms of commitment are to be viewed as derivative and relative. Any theology of religious life which subverts this primacy of baptism stands on weak ground. To make religious vows, not baptismal vows, the ultimate reference point in evaluating our existential commitments, is a reversal of Gospel priorities. Similarly, as John Coleman has shown, to center one's vision and strategies for fulfillment of the Church's mission around the sacrament of orders and not around the sacrament of baptism is to displace the center of apostolic gravity within the Christian community.

Second, neither religious vows nor commitment to priestly office are thereby deprived of their special dignity and giftedness. Religious life, in the immense variety of its historical forms, remains in this view a striking manifestation of the working of the Spirit at the grassroots of the Church. Provided the argument is made carefully and with full respect for the primacy of the baptismal commitment, and allowing for the freedom of the Spirit to create today charismatic communities in which the three traditional vows are not essential structures, it makes sense to view in religious communities a special charismatic, prophetic, sacramental, countercultural, or eschatological quality, as most theologies of religious life maintain. Similarly, though Vatican II's language of a difference in essence and not merely in degree between the priesthood of the baptized and the priesthood of the ordained is probably dated, the structure of priestly office remains important, so that the call to office continues to be a significant element in the total vocation of a Christian and religious.

Still, there is room for considerable variety with respect to the importance of the call to office in the life of this or that Jesuit. I have found it enlightening in recent years to put to fellow Jesuits the question, "If you had to choose between continuing to function as a priest, on condition that you leave the Society of Jesus, and, on the other hand, continuing to be a Jesuit, on condition that you not exercise priestly office, which would you choose?" Though the question is not an actual one, it can serve to help us relate and evaluate the facets of our commitment. Different Jesuit priests answer it differently, some hesitantly, some more firmly. I am of the latter group. At this stage of my life, though the exercise of the priestly office, especially in the celebration of the Eucharist when my services are required, consoles me, I have no doubt that my being a Jesuit represents a deeper aspect of God's call to me than my being an ordained priest. In the unlikely event of being confronted with the mentioned choice, my choice would be to continue as a Jesuit, in a vocation which would be practically identical with that of the Jesuit brother.

As I see it, such a choice would not put me in contradiction with the historical situation of the Society of Jesus as a body within the presbyterate and with a special relationship to the bishop of Rome. If the vast majority of Jesuit priests, however, make a similar choice, a major tension would result for our traditional role as presbyters and as linked within the presbyterate with the Roman Pontiff. Practically speaking, such an eventuality is not worth considering.

On the other hand, the presbyteral character of the Society of Jesus as a whole does not exclude that it be conceived as a community in which lay and clerical Christians commit themselves to share a vowed apostolic life. This was not, indeed, the original conception of the Society of Jesus, because the basic differentiating structure was the distinction between solemnly professed (always priest) and coadjutors (some lay, some priests). But the lay/clerical conception is not excluded by the original structure, which has become largely irrelevant, and in today's cultural context appears a more operative version of Jesuit apostolic identity.

All of this leads me, in summary, to endorse the language of a recent statement by the National Jesuit Brothers' Committee:

> The radical vocation of all Jesuits is to apostolic service. This is foundational to all Jesuit programs. The ministries of the Society involve both ordained and lay religious. Consequently, we can talk about our shared or corporate apostolic vocation, with two specifications of how that vocation can be fulfilled, i.e. as a cleric or lay religious. [7]

Whatever abstract or juridical distinctions may remain from the origins and history of the Society of Jesus, I believe that today our most promising self-image is that of apostolic, Ignatian men, lay and clerical, committed to participation in the mission of the Church, especially as this mission is directed to the transformation of society. From this perspective, the presence of lay Christians within our membership is crucial to our corporate fulfillment of the Ignatian charism as a mysticism of apostolic service in the world. If the empowerment of the laity is, as I believe it to be, a key to the fulfillment of the Church's mission of transformation of the world, then the envisaging of Jesuit community as an apostolic collaboration of lay and clerical Christians offers a perspective radically different from one in which Jesuit brothers would be seen merely as pragmatic supports for a ministry exclusively defined in terms of ordained priesthood. It is true that many, perhaps most, Jesuit brothers, not to speak of Jesuit priests and scholastics, are unaccustomed to consider the brothers as members of the laity; the prevailing language among us had tended to see brothers somewhat as the Tridentine Church saw women religious, as a middle group situated between real laity and clergy. But we are not condemned to perpetuate such a view, and, with some inconsistency, Vatican II's Constitution on the Church provides an explicit base for seeing Jesuit brothers as members of the laity. [8]

Implicit in the preceding paragraphs is a "theology of religious life," considered not abstractly, but in the concrete historical identity of one particular community, the Jesuits. I recall hearing Alan McCoy, past president of CMSM, say that there is no such *thing* as religious life. Few indeed are the transcendental elements common to all the historical communities which have been so designated. What I have highlighted here, at this historical juncture for the Jesuit community, is the primacy of the vowed life common to all baptized Christians, the apostolic and "worldly" character of the Jesuit vocation, shared by lay and clerical members, and the importance of that "sign of the times" which is the emergence of the laity in the Church's mission of transforming society. These are basic components of *a* theology of religious life in the Society of Jesus. Other Jesuits will construct other theologies of the life they share, and members of other communities will construct their own theologies, respecting the different charisms, histories, and present situations. At least for purposes of the pastoral circle, this appears to be as much as is possible or necessary to say by way of providing a theology of religious life which may help to evaluate the present situation of brothers within clerical communities.

This lengthy exercise of evaluation within the third stage of the pastoral circle will unfortunately overshadow the equally necessary exercise of what I have called revisioning, or the imaginative exploration of alternatives to the present situation. Space constraints preclude lengthy treatment of this important activity. When evaluation has disclosed that the present situation falls short of gospel criteria, Christian imagination needs to be enlisted by conceiving alternative scenarios for our life together. A few examples in the present context: what would it be like if we were to widen the scope of delegated power carried by a brother who serves as minister within a local community; or if we were to encourage the practice, when brothers or other lay people are present, of having a single priest, without concelebrants, presiding at the Eucharist; or if, in Jesuit parishes, a brother were appointed to be the administrator or actual pastor of the community, while available Jesuit priests fulfilled the roles for which ordination is required?

This phase of theological reflection calls for an openness to new ideas on the part of the entire group, and for the suspension of critical judgment long enough to let dreaming imagination exercise its distinctive power.

In summary, the third phase of the pastoral circle, theological reflection in a narrow sense, took some aspects of the experienced and analyzed situation of brothers in clerical communities, subjected this to evaluation on the basis of Gospel criteria, and then, to the extent to which the present situation was found wanting, searched for creative alternatives. The emergence of such alternatives brings the process to its fourth and final phase.

IV. Discerning Pastoral Decision

THE FOURTH PHASE of the pastoral circle brings the process to decision and action. Here again a sharp difference from magisterial and academic ways in theology emerges. Christian decision is no longer a mere consequence of the process but a constitutive element. Faith finds the understanding that it seeks only within the action which it informs. One of the values of this paradigm for theologizing on the place of brothers in clerical communities is that it discountenances endless and sterile discussion. It says: You will not really understand what you are talking about until you concretize your understanding in responsible action.

The theologizing group, then, brings towards decision the social situation it has experienced, analyzed, evaluated, and revisioned. At this point the pervasive influence of faith as responsive to the movement of God's Spirit in the group and its members becomes newly prominent. It is true that recourse to prayer, especially with the help of the Scriptures or of the Eucharistic celebration, may be appropriate at other stages of the process. And concern for faithfulness to the Spirit needs to be continuous, lest diffidence, self-interest, or cultural attachments vitiate the exercise of story, analysis, evaluation and revisioning. Still, it is in the immediate adjuncts of decision that the danger of "inordinate affections" and the necessity of inner freedom become manifest. At this point, too, the clarity required by a sound spiritual decision is an exigency.

Fortunately, the recent revival of the theology and spirituality of the traditional "discernment of spirits" will help any group seeking clarity and freedom in making significant choices. Without offering a detailed method, here are some of the "spiritual exercises" in which a group can now engage with a view to pastoral decision.

First, each member of the group can be asked to pray and reflect privately on where he experiences confusion or lack of freedom regarding what the group is considering. It will help if each individual is in touch with the source of confusion or lack of freedom, for example whether it stems from a personal history which has led to unresolved fears and angers, or from cultural assumptions which he shares with other priests, other brothers. If I am a priest, I can ask: What really goes on in my daily relationships with brothers within my community? Do I have to reckon with my own defensiveness or hidden assumptions of superiority? Do I fear that somehow the spiritual strength I derive from functioning as an ordained minister is being threatened? If I am a brother, comparable questions will be in order. How, through prayer and open dialogue, can we keep such inner troublings and confinements from impeding our full participation in a truly free group decision?

Second, the group as a whole may wish to return to the cultural aspects of the analysis already made, so as to come to a common sense of the cultural stereotypes and pressures which might make the decision reactive rather than responsive and responsible. Cultural tides and groundswells are legitimate factors in communal decision-making, and for an important dimension of the ''signs of the times'' through which the Spirit moves the Church in times of change. But we are admonished not to trust every such movement or sign but to test it, to see if it is coming from God (1 John 4:1)

Third, clarity is a primary value in group discernment. While it is not fully reducible to rational clarity, its intuitive character must be balanced with as much objectivity as is feasible. The discernment of spirits differs greatly from the use of a Ouija board or the consultation of I Ching tables!

Fourth, through prayer and mutual support the group needs to remain in the basic posture of seeking always God's presence and God's will. Peace, joy, hope, harmony, when they abide despite differences of opinion, they are all but infallible signs that good decisions are in the making. I say good decisions, not necessarily correct decisions. Given our human fallibility, we have no guarantee that, several miles down the road, we will not look back with regret at important decisions which turned out to be incorrect. But a community can survive incorrect decisions, even many of them, provided its decisional experiences have been characterized by awareness, freedom, and a basic communion.

By way of conclusion, let me return to my very first statement, that this chapter would not offer *a* theology of the relationships of brothers and priests within religious communities so much as a method or process by which groups might dialogue with a view to discerning decisions. My own decision to proceed in this way has been a deliberate one, and stems from the conviction that the best energies for shaping our life together come not from professionals but from groups within our communities. I hope that the sketch of the pastoral circle which I have here provided will encourage such groups to engage in this kind of theology.

As a final word — and as a gesture towards the kind of essay I have *not* written — I would propose that in any such group reflection the priest-brother relationship be considered within a larger challenge: the pastoral imperative of empowering of the laity of the Church for their full share in mission and ministry. In my opinion it would be myopic to deal with the domestic problem which engages us in this volume without acknowledging its linkage with the larger pastoral problem which confronts the Church. Declericalizing our communities in their inner structures and cultural climates needs to be viewed as a dimension of the larger declericalization of the life of the Church to which all of us are called. Declericalization does not mean, of course, that we seek to create a Church bereft of specific offices of leadership. But we do need to disengage from cultural mindsets and climates which are not fully faithful to the Gospel call to shared discipleship, within the basic equality and communion which are ours through baptism and confirmation.

Endnotes

1 T. Clarke, "A New Way: Reflecting on Experience," in: J. Hug, *Tracing The Spirit: Spiritual and Pastoral Models*, Kansas City: Sheed & Ward, 1986, p. 161. See also J. Holland & P. Henriot, *Social Analysis: Linking Faith and Justice*, Maryknoll: Orbis, 1980, and R. Hofbauer, D. Kinsella, A. Miller, *Making Social Analysis Useful*, Washington, D.C.: Leadership Conference of Women Religious, 1983.

2 *Poems and Prose*, Baltimore: Penguin, 1970, pp. 66f.

3 *The Total Development of the Jesuit Brother: Assistancy Conference, August 17-19, 1969*, Santa Clara, CA: University of Santa Clara, 1969 (unpublished notes), p. 15.

4 J. Padberg, "The Society True to Itself: A Brief History of the 32nd General Congregation of the Society of Jesus (December 2, 1974 - March 7, 1975)," *Studies in the
   Spirituality of Jesuits* 15 (1983), nos. 3 & 4.
5 G. Ganss, "Towards Understanding the Jesuit Brothers' Vocation, especially as
   described in the Papal and Jesuit Documents." *Studies in the Spirituality of Jesuits* 13
   (1981), no. 3.
6 Vatican II, *Decree on the Appropriate Renewal of Religious Life*, n. 3, tr. W. Abbott & J.
   Gallagher, *The Documents of Vatican II*, New York: America Press, 1966, p. 469.
7 "The Jesuit Brother: A Statement by the National Jesuit Brothers' Committee to American Jesuits," p. 2 (unpublished statement).
8 The *Dogmatic Constitution on the Church* teaches that the religious state is not a middle
   state between those of laity and clergy and that, in fact, it does not belong to the
   hierarchical structure of the Church (nos. 33, 34). Yet earlier, the same document defines
   laity so as to exclude not only clergy but also religious (n. 31).

Brothers and Priests as Confreres

MARTIN HELLDORFER, F.S.C

L IVING AS A LAY BROTHER in the twentieth century is a healthy, productive and valuable way to live. It is also a dangerous way. The danger lies in the climate surrounding the lifestyle.

I use the word climate hesitantly but deliberately because it conveys a sense of gathering together various elements such as temperature, wind, and precipitation in order to communicate a sense of what it is like to live in a particular place. The word also refers to conditions measured over a long period of time. The experience at a specific location on a particular day is only one element in the larger picture. Brothers live in a climate that is dangerous; specific brothers in particular places are exceptions.

While the lifestyle is dangerous, it is also privileged. Persons who are called and who choose to live as brothers have a unique opportunity not only to serve others, but also to live happy and personally fulfilling lives.

This chapter will focus on an analysis of the climate. It begins with the way things were, proceeds to describe the present moment, and concludes with a section outlining the issues that brothers face in the future. The reflections are written in a style that evokes discussion.

On the Way Things Were

IN THE RELATIVELY recent past, previous to Vatican II, the brothers' lifestyle struggled under the weight of six problems.

The Problem of Identity

When someone says of another, "He's a fireman," we know who he is. We have words and categories that place the individual in a context understood by all. The person has a social identity. That identity tends to be given by others rather than created by the individual. Take away that identity and the individual flounders.

The brothers identity was a non-identity. Church law and common parlance referred to them as "non-clerics." To be identified in terms of what one is not, is to consider oneself in reference to what one does not have. In the case of the brothers, what was missing was ordination.

At first glance, to speak of identity in terms of what is missing does not seem particularly important. However, to glimpse its significance, consider the way in which female sexuality was understood during the early years of psychiatry. During those pioneer times, the writers were male medical doctors. When they spoke of female sexuality they did so from the perspective of their own experiences as males and as medical doctors. They spoke of female sexuality in a negative form indicating that the women in general suffered from an inferiority complex because the feminine organs were incomplete when compared with the male organs. They claimed that a woman yearned for what she did not have.

The jury is still out regarding the accuracy of this aspect of unconscious sexuality, but there is little doubt regarding the effects of speaking of female sexuality in terms of what is missing. It has taken decades for the profession to realize that what it thought was so important is not so important in the experience of women about whom they theorized. Phrased another way, women have their own sexual experience, their own sexual identity, and their own sense of value. To speak of them in terms of what they do not have is to speak unknowingly from a perspective of power and even arrogance.

Brothers were in a position similar to that of women in a bygone age. They were not understood in a positive sense but rather in a negative way when compared with the ordained clergy. Who were brothers? They were men who were not ordained. Not only did clergy speak in this way; brothers did as well. From a psychological perspective, that was a dangerous atmosphere in which to live. It was a climate that bred self-doubt. What was, is still present in some situations today.

A Structural Problem

Social structure shapes individual experience and behavior. For instance, being the only, youngest, middle or oldest child in a family creates recurring patterns of behavior that are recognized from family to family. Or, to use another example, consider the resentment that often builds between wives and mothers-in-law. The jaundiced eye of one toward the other rises in part because of the structure into which they are cast.

Brothers were situated in a hierarchically constituted structure. Clerics were higher than brothers. In practice, this meant that brothers could not hold authority positions over the ordained. Men could become priests; the ordained could not become brothers. At that period in Church history, many persons asked young men and brothers, ''Why don't you go all the way and become priests?'' The question was asked seriously. It would have been humorous to ask ordained persons why they did not go all the way to become brothers. No one would have understood.

The structure induced resentment. One had only to be among brothers for a short time to hear the anticlerical tone surrounding their stories. Living in that climate, men soon felt that they were *only* brothers. That self-devalued stance did not develop solely because men suffered from serious intrapsychic unresolved conflicts from their youths. The problem was a structural one. The effects of the structural problem were intensified in those communities where brothers were told by their confreres that they were equal. To the degree that equality was stated but withheld, to that degree were men immobilized.

Resentful feelings are dangerous. They color perception and poison the tongue. They lead persons to devalue the world rather than to care for it. Such feelings do not lead toward effective ministry, supportive relationships, or healthy self-acceptance.

Community and Intimacy

A third problem rose from the manner in which brothers and priests lived together.

The brothers' community set out to provide for all of their needs. Room, board, employment, and even a place of retirement, were offered. There was little need to go outside of the community for anything. Even friendships, insofar as they were encouraged, were expected to be with confreres within the community setting.

The same ideal was presented to those who were ordained but the practice was different. Most priests had ministerial contacts outside of the community. That same involvement provided men with the opportunity to develop a network of friends and acquaintances that knowingly satisfied many personal needs. For the ordained, the ministry was often the sustaining element in their lives. Many would say, ''I could leave the community but I could not easily leave the ministry.''

The situation was different for the brothers. Their role was often to care for the physical maintenance of buildings, to look after the kitchen or to offer clerical assistance, and thereby to participate in the principal work of the Order which was usually a sacramental ministry. The brothers' contacts with the world apart from the community or institution were minimal. Their lives were understimulated. Priests who were affected both positively and negatively by the ministry returned to the community as a resting place to prepare for the next day. They needed privacy when they returned. Brothers, who generally worked alone and whose lives were circumscribed by the community during the day, needed companionship when their day was finished. Both groups developed overly private lifestyles within the community setting. Brothers developed particularly isolated lifestyles. In that situation men were often troubled by sexual phantasies and scrupulosity. Brothers sometimes developed not only a fear of women, but of closeness to men, and of involvement with the world apart from the community. As idiosyncrasies became marked in later life, the behaviors were said to result from the fact that the men were not particularly gifted. Little attention was given to the influence of their lifestyle.

The Problem of the Workplace

In recent years, many religious prayed, ate, slept and even relaxed in the same building in which they worked. They lived, as it were, above the store. That physical arrangement could be likened to workers constructing a building during the day while sleeping in a corner of that same structure at night. Generally speaking, it is not a healthy living arrangement.

When brothers lived in the relatively closed circle of the community or institution in which they worked, the problems were intensified. One such problem was the way in which brothers' interests were narrowed. Suppose a man had a gift for carpentry. Suppose, too, that he lived above the store. That living arrangement would soon narrow his interests, especially if he was affirmed in his work and enjoyed what he was doing. Over a period of time he would be inclined to say to himself, "I really like my work.

There is nothing I would rather do.'' And he would feel just the way he spoke. If the ballet was in town, he was not interested. A movie could be very popular, but interest was not pricked. If there was a theological controversy he avoided it. At community meetings he had little to say. He had his own interests which kept him occupied and usually on the job.

In pre-Vatican II days such a lifestyle was eulogized. Others could say of brothers, ''What good men they are. How simple and how devoted.'' The intended compliment masked both personal and communal problems. Those problems were seen when religious life changed and when men were invited to reconsider their ministries. Many brothers could not respond to the invitation because their interests had become so narrowed. If they had options, they did not know what they were. I once heard a provincial superior at a public meeting of other provincials say that the only brothers who remained in his Order were the ones with problems. He spoke of them as ''leftovers from a bygone age'' and advocated that his Order should no longer accept men as brothers. The problem that he wanted to solve was caused, in part, by having gifted men live isolatedly ''above the store.''

The Problem of Being Called a "Lay" Brother

The use of the word ''lay'' arose at a time when those who were educated to read and write were called clerics. Those who were not educated were called laymen. Educated men were often ordained and consequently known as the clergy. The unskilled were laymen.

We use similar distinctions today. For instance, when a medical doctor refers to a legal issue, we say that he speaks as a layperson. The use of the word conveys a sense of being unskilled relative to a particular field of expertise. Brothers were called lay, not in the context of another talent, but as a title to define who they were.

No insult was intended. The word was used in a technical canonical sense. Few brothers were even consciously aware of the devalued stance in which they were placed. Even today, ordained persons find it difficult to appreciate the feelings surrounding the use of the word. There are at least two reasons for this: first, when we are in a favored stance, the devalued position is seldom offensive. Few white people intended insult when referring to persons as negroes. Secondly, this decade's use of the word "lay" has positive connotations. It is difficult to appreciate the feelings surrounding the use of the word in the past. That is because it has shifted in its meaning similar to the way other words such as "black" or "Irish" have changed from being derogatory terms to valued qualities. In pre-Vatican II days within clergy circles, laymen were looked down upon in not-so-conscious ways as persons without authority, knowledge or power within the Church. A glance at the literature of the period reflects the struggle.

When being a brother and being unskilled were linked, the climate favored the formation of dutiful, quiet, hard working, and even self-deprecating individuals. The brothers' spirituality reinforced the problem. It stressed hidden, humble service. Holiness was associated with acceptance of God's will. In reality that meant acceptance of the way things were done.

The above-mentioned dynamics operated largely outside the world of awareness. However, at that period of history men were conscious that being a lay brother situated them in a position between the clergy and laity. The priests excluded brothers from their fraternal gatherings and from many decision-making processes. On the other side, layperson considered brothers members of the clergy. Everyone knew that a brother was not really a layman. As a result, brothers lived between the two groups. They were unseen and seldom acknowledged notwithstanding the fact that there were more than 15,000 brothers in the United States in the decades immediately before Vatican II.

This in-between place was an unsettling space in which to live unless individuals had strong fraternal support and firm personal identities. Generally, all-brother groups found such support and identity more easily than their confreres in clerical communities.

The Problem of Past Discernment Procedures

In practice, the decision to become a brother or priest in clerical Orders was determined in part by the measure of a man's analytical intelligence. Those who had the ability to pursue university level studies (theologate) were encouraged to seek ordination. Those not so gifted became brothers. Consequently, as a group, priests were smarter and more highly educated. Formation programs, educational experiences, and the consequent development of differing interests, separated the men into two groups. Whether at table, in front of the television or at meetings, the groups were clearly distinct. In the climate of those days, intelligence was overvalued among the clergy and devalued among the brothers. The stereotypes of the day reflected the problem: priests were heady and brothers were dull. Again, the climate was dangerous. If a young man was struggling with identity and intimacy issues when he entered an Order — a struggle that is age-appropriate for many men — then the atmosphere of the community was challenging at best.

* * *   *   * * *

IN SUMMARY, the identity problem facilitated a feeling of unsureness. The structural problem induced resentment. The community problem fostered isolation. The workplace problem helped create a depressive atmosphere and a sense of helplessness. The designation "lay" situated the brothers between groups and obliquely devalued them. Self-deprecating behavior followed. The discernment problem polarized communities and fanned an individual's sense of being inferior.

The above-mentioned dynamics are confirmed by reviewing the psychological literature associated with assessment procedures for candidates to religious life. For example, psychologists frequently used the *16 Personality Factor Questionnaire (16PF)* to help discern the advisability of accepting an applicant into religious life. The test measured sixteen personality factors which formed patterns that were then correlated with vocational choice. The thought was that persons with this or that behavioral pattern would fit into groups that had congruent patterns. The clinical *Handbook* printed in 1970, spoke of the profile of priests, seminarians, and brothers in the following manner.

> The Roman Catholic priest profile deviates from the general population only moderately, but in a very specific way and with high statistical significance in the 1707 cases. It is consistently inviant except for below-average self-sufficiency. It is also consistently on the anxious side, but particularly so in guilt proneness. An outstanding feature is the very high premsia (I), suggesting a protected emotional sensitivity in childhood. . . .
>
> Compared to the priest-monk group just described, the seminarians are a decidedly more exviant and less anxious group, though otherwise generally similar. . . .

When the text described the profile of brothers, it stated that the

> . . . personality pattern of brothers shows humble conformity, with shyness, ego weakness, submissiveness, and conservatism. (p. 221).

Clearly, the brother's lifestyle was portrayed negatively. Perhaps such a characterization was a bias. If it were, that same bias seems present today. For instance, an authoritative study of stress among religious leaders which appeared in a 1986 issue of *The Journal of Clinical Psychology* ends with the following remarks:

> The brothers seemed to be the most unaware and least sensitive about the issues raised on the Religious and Stress Questionnaire. Perhaps this was due to their leaning toward ultra-conservatism; noncommitment with regard to matters not immediately within their purview; their being unaware or insensitive to the issues; their being unrealistic; their not really caring about social and personal issues of concern outside their immediate context of the classroom or the hospital setting, even though such matters were serious topics and situations within the larger context of their denomination; or they may have found the area very stressful and used a plausible excuse for not dealing with such issues. Further study with an even larger sample would help resolve some of these questions.

> (Rayburn, Carole A.; Richmond, Lee J. and Rogers, Lynn. *Journal of Clinical Psychology*, 1986 (May), Vol. 42(3), 540-546.)

Given the date of the research it appears that the same negative view of our lifestyle seems to endures. Whether an accurate or biased view of the brothers, it seems to me that many men have lived maturely and vibrantly as brothers within this seemingly dangerous climate. Personally, I believe that I have met and sometimes lived with persons who could only be described as extraordinary.

On the Way Things Are

THE WAY THINGS ARE is not the way things were. Vatican II, either actually or by metaphor, represents a turning point in the history of religious life and of the brothers. The Council either caused, allowed or forced the brothers to face the contemporary culture from which they were protected. This process is still taking place.

To describe what it is to be a brother today is perhaps best captured by telling the story of the Elephant Man.

The Elephant Man is a play in which the central figure is a grotesquely deformed person who meets a beautiful woman. Both change each other remarkably. In telling the story, I am likening the brothers to the Elephant Man and the woman to the culture. My purpose is to convey a felt sense of what has happened to brothers and how it feels to be a brother. My contention is that the situation of the brothers can be understood as a love-story between brothers and the contemporary culture.

The play opens with a description of the Elephant Man. His head is monstrous, resembling an elephant's. A gaping hole marks the place of the man's mouth and a lump of flesh forms his nose. One arm and both legs are horribly misshapen. Only his left arm and genitals are normal. The arm that is not deformed is so delicately shaped that it could be mistaken for a woman's. A stench surrounds him and his voice is garbled. He offends every sense.

A doctor and an actress take an interest in him. The doctor sees the man as an "interesting case" and the actress feels that she is doing "good" by extending herself. The play portrays the developing relationship between the Elephant Man and the actress.

There are two particularly moving moments in the play which involve touch. The first is when the Elephant Man and the actress are parting after their first meeting. In preparation for that visit, the doctor had showed the actress anatomical photographs of the Elephant Man and carefully instructed her on how to avoid embarrassing the man by forcing him to expose his deformities. The doctor told her to extend her left, not her right, hand when greeting him. "After all," he said, "you do not want to embarrass him." It was his left hand that was so ugly.

They met as planned but when about to leave, tenderly and deliberately, the actress removed the glove from her right hand, not the left as she had been prompted to do. Both know what is being expressed. At that moment when flesh touches flesh, boundaries are crossed and rules are broken. The act to be avoided becomes the act to be done. What is proper becomes shallow. What was discouraged becomes meaningful. In that meeting the Elephant Man discovers the woman behind the do-gooder and she finds a sensitive man behind his deformities.

As the play develops, so does the closeness between the two. The woman's sensitivity is a special gift to the man; his wisdom is an offering to her. After quite a long time of increasing closeness, he wants just one thing: to make love with the woman he adores.

He asks. She responds ''no'' with her words but ''yes'' with her heart. Both fear the moment. Standing some distance from him she unbuttons her dress and lets it fall to her waist. Her pale and beautifully formed body is exposed. He stares in amazement and struggles for words. ''Beautiful,'' he murmurs, ''the most beautiful sight I have ever seen.''

In that intense moment the doctor enters the room and discovers the woman standing half-naked before the Elephant Man. ''What is this?'' he yells. ''What are you doing?'' His words condemn what they know as good. The woman is embarrassed and can only clutch at her dress. No words are possible. There is nothing to be said. The silence is not of union but of bewilderment.

That is what has happened to the brothers. We, like the Elephant Man, have loved. He was changed by his unplanned relationship with the woman. Our love relationship is not with a woman, but with our culture. We have left the monastery and entered the marketplace. It is attractive and valuable. When faced with its beauty, past practices and rules are shaken. As a group, the brothers' feelings reflect the Elephant Man's: *bewilderment, attraction, fear, goodness, appreciation, guilt, care, hope, construction* and even *tragedy*. Without an awareness of these feelings it is difficult to appreciate the experience of the brother in today's Church.

In the play, the Elephant Man was broken by the doctor's condemnation. The story ends tragically. With a deliberation comparable to that of the actress when she first removed the glove from her right hand, the Elephant Man walks over to his bed and lies down in such a manner that his enlarged head hangs unsupported from the mattress. He dies of asphyxiation.

It is unlikely that the brothers will choose the same fate. I know of no group of brothers who have decided to die. I do know of groups in which the clerics have made a decision not to accept men as brothers. From a psychological perspective, this approach to solving the problem reflects the brother-cleric conflict in the extreme; that is, a decision is made for the men concerned rather than by the men themselves.

Today, brothers are in crisis. They are facing an attractive though disconcerting contemporary world. The closer they approach that world, the more they are changed. As brothers come to appreciate the culture's values and needs, they hear the same condemnatory voices that the Elephant Man heard. "What are you doing?" Not only do they hear those words from others; they arise within their own hearts as well. Today, brothers tred on dangerous ground. The past climate was dangerous; the present is no less so.

The ordained do not experience the love relationship with the contemporary world in the same way as the brothers. They are moved into ministry with an agenda; namely, to evangelize. The ministry is a buffer. Their message says in so many differing ways, "There is another Kingdom, there is much more to life than that which appears." Many brothers do not have such an agenda unless their ministry is directly associated with the proclamation of the gospel. Those who are "lay" such as teachers, researchers, cooks, chemists, clinicians, plumbers, technicians, or artists have no buffer between themselves and what Church persons call the "world." This is an extraordinary difference from the standpoint of experience between brothers and ordained ministers. Brothers live with questions such as "Why are we brothers?" and "What makes us different from others?" Brothers do not have a special power whose exercise is reserved to them alone. That is precisely the brothers' gift and why their presence is so important in our Church and culture.

On the Way Things May Be

BROTHERS ARE CHANGING. New lifestyles are being forged. No one knows the future but there is reason to believe that its contours will be shaped by the way brothers face today's problems. Again, those problems can be understood as involving a love relationship with the contemporary world. What is so attractive and so disconcerting about that world that is loved? It has to do with its beauty and its values; specifically material things, sex and autonomy.

Things. We relish the work of our hands. We value what we build. The world we love loves things. The Western technological world is a place of abundance, not for everyone, but for many. We like our televisions, computers, art, foods, fine homes, and what have been called the good things of life.

Sex. The world we love values sex. It particularly values sexual expressions of affection within loving relationships. Withholding such expression is viewed with suspicion. Why, our contemporaries say, would anyone ever want to be celibate? Brothers ask themselves the same question.

Autonomy. Our contemporaries value independence, initiative and personal responsibility. Dependence, especially when blind, is repulsive to the world we love. Why forfeit one's ability to shape one's own life? That leads not only to mediocrity but to major psychological problems.

Brothers who move closer and closer to the world (as indeed, it is their calling to do) are influenced by it. Today, they find themselves face to face with its attractive ways. Brothers have their computers, credit cards, and checking accounts. Given the world in which they live, they wonder about the value of poverty. As unsettling as it is, they sometimes find themselves in relationships where they ask why they should refrain from the sexual expression of love. When they hear voices of authority that seem to echo the words of the intrusive doctor, ''What are you doing?'' they also question the value of obedience. All of this is a way of saying that the brothers must articulate a spirituality for the present age, the here and now.

Reshaping spirituality is not a process unknown in the history of the Church. Augustine, Benedict, Francis, Ignatius and others: each rewrote the understanding of the vows in their centuries. Perhaps future historians will look back on our time and note how sisters and brothers did the same for our age by finding a way to live *appreciatively* (poverty) in a world that was troubled by an acquisitive posture; *respectively* (chastity) in a world that noticed groups rather than individuals; *openly* (obedience) not only to superiors, but to everyone no matter how hesitant the voice.

In the recent past, the brothers spoke of the need for detachment from this world's goods. That message is not needed today. Distance, isolation and detachment are actually our problems. In this century, we need a spirituality of attachment. To illustrate, consider the following experience. I know a layman who is a competent administrator and fine clinician. He was recently awarded a sabbatical year and in the process of readying himself for travel, he had to divest himself of many responsibilities — not only in the workplace but at home as well. He needed to find persons to open his mail, make bank deposits, collect rents, pay bills, keep his dog, and so on. On the last day of work he came to the staff meeting and said he had never felt so ''light'' in his life. He was almost giddy after having divested himself and he said that he thought he knew what the monks of old were trying to tell us about poverty.

He was right. The problem is that in recent history brothers have tried to discover the value of detachment (poverty) before becoming attached.

Also, the recent past, the brothers spoke of the need to be selfless, free of personal relationships, and ready to be of service. Neither is that message needed today. The effects of loneliness and isolation are our problems. We need to develop a spirituality that values loving relationships. Little more needs to be said about this. We know the problems that arise when men are isolated. The challenge is to let loving relationships surface at a time when they are viewed with suspicion.

In the recent past, the brothers spoke of the need to relinquish their will in an effort to participate in the mission of their community. That message is not needed today. Passivity, dependence and depression are problems. We need to develop a spirituality that values interdependence. Such a spirituality implies remarkably strong and self-determining individuals.

I know a man who was told by his provincial that he was needed in a fund-raising office of his Order. The man thanked his superior for letting him know of the need and then added that he found it necessary to take some time before accepting the position. Specifically he wanted to listen (obedience) to what others had to say before accepting the position. The man thought of obedience in terms of listening to everyone, including the superior. In fact, much to the disappointment of many he did not accept the position. That way of living certainly does not fit the pattern of "humble conformity, with shyness, ego weakness and submissiveness" that seemingly characterized a past personality type of men who became brothers.

Brothers value community life. If they are to move into the future, they must deal with a serious contemporary problem; namely, how to live within many communities. As brothers move out of their supportive institutional roles, they discover that they belong to many communities. One might be the community of their colleagues, another their family, a third, friends, and still a fourth might be their worshipping community. Soon the community back home can become a resting place, similar to the way that community is lived by some ordained persons whose ministries have engaged their primary interests and whose energies for the community are minimal. The brothers must find a way to live vibrantly in community while being intensely involved with the world apart from it.

Lastly, and perhaps most importantly, the task that faces brothers today is to speak out. Until now, their voices have not been heard. As mentioned above, the brothers' situation can be likened to that of women in bygone days when men tried to speak for them. No one, including the brothers, will know who they are until they speak. Speaking is a theological task. It is creative and prophetic insofar as words form the world that will be. If brothers remain silent, their lifestyle and the climate surrounding it, will remain dangerous. As they speak, it will likely become evident that living as a brother in this particular moment of history is a healthy, productive and valuable way to live. As always, the question is one of discernment, calling and response.

Canon Law:
Rights and Relationships

JUSTIN DER, O.F.M., Cap.

T HE CHALLENGE issued by Vatican II to religious institutes to renew themselves is still being pursued by religious. An important concern in male institutes with both lay and clerical members is the variation and status of lay members. Revisions of constitutions have taken place or are in the process of revision. Added to this is the state of crisis that has afflicted many religious institutes within the last decade as they face declining numbers and a search for identity. "The crisis has been one of significance, or worthwhileness, of identity. . . . The crisis for many brothers, especially those who are members of what the revised Code of Canon Law terms 'clerical institutes,' is one relating to their finality and value. More traumatic for many brothers than the large reduction in their numbers worldwide has been their struggle to be recognized, affirmed, and acknowledged as a significant presence within the Church."[1]

Questions have been raised in recent years concerning the very existence of this class of religious, as if one were to question the need or rationale for a separate class of religious men within the framework of an order or a congregation. Questions are also raised concerning the role of the brother in the institute and his participation in the internal life of the society in which he has vowed his life. In fact, the brother in most clerical orders or congregations is looked upon as somewhat of an anomaly by a society which regards advancement and progression in status as realistic goals, whether in the religious, the secular, or the intellectual world.[2]

For the last several centuries the general law of the Church has maintained a uniform subordination of the lay members to the clerical members in religious institutes in which both classes of membership may be found. It is not the sacrament of Orders that determines a hierarchy within the religious states, but rather the constitutions of the various religious societies that provided for the distinction of the members into various classes. In many institutes the founders made little distinction between clerical and non-clerical members and in the early days of some orders no hierarchy of membership existed. The distinction in membership came about partially as a result of the legislation of the Church and from the institutes themselves. At times these distinctions were brought about because of the pressing needs of the Church in a given period, the exigencies of evangelization, or in response to abuses which crept into the religious life at various historical moments. It is important to note, however, that the division into classes is not essential to the nature of the mission of the religious life, and that such division was not envisioned in the earliest rules of life.[3]

The Second Vatican Council has led all religious institutes to re-evaluate their life and spirit, to study the gifts that their religious institutes bring to the Church universal, and to the charism(s) that caused their founding. Each religious institute has been asked by the Council and by Pontiffs to examine the totality of their life in religion and to adapt, modify, renew and re-invigorate their witness to the Church and to the world. The Council in the Decree *Perfectae Caritatis* stated: "In the Church there are many institutes, clerical and lay, engaged in different kinds of apostolic work and endowed with gifts which vary according to the grace that is given to them. . . . Since the active religious life takes many forms, this diversity should be taken into account when its up-to-date renewal is being undertaken, and in the various institutes the members' life of service of Christ should be sustained by means which are proper and suitable to each institute."[4]

The same document takes up a thread of this argument in another section. "In order to strengthen the bond of brotherhood between the members of an institute, those who are called brothers, cooperators, or some such name should be associated more closely with the life and work of the community. . . . Men's monasteries and institutes which are not entirely lay can, of their very nature, admit clerics and laymen, in accordance with the constitutions, on an equal footing and with equal rights and obligations, apart from those arising out of sacred orders."[5]   The Council, then, gave the impetus to all orders and congregations to renew their legislation and to evaluate how faithful they were to the mind, the spirit, the ideals of their founders, and the traditions of the institutes.

The revised Code of Canon Law, promulgated in 1983, gives another impetus to religious institutes to renew themselves in accord with the mind of the Church. The Code takes into account the decrees of the Council and the subsequent enabling legislation. "Flexibility, subsidiarity, respect for a wide range of traditions and charisms: all this came to be successfully incorporated in the new law on institutes of consecrated life and societies of apostolic life. . . . Above all, the importance of the proper law of the institute is guaranteed, assuring the continuation of the founder's unique vision, charism and gifts."[6]

Several canons of the Code address the issue of the particular charism that the Church recognizes in each institute and of the need to preserve, sustain, and maintain this gift of the Spirit, and inheritance of their founders. Canon 577 states: "There are many institutes of consecrated life, with gifts that differ according to the graces given them. . . ."[7]   The founders of religious orders and congregations had, in common, the desire for a total response to the gospel. "Thus it is that each group of religious sets in motion particular means of personal sanctification, of witness and of action, and is received by the community of believers as a sign different from the others."[8]

Canon 578 declares: "The intention of the founders and their determination concerning the nature, purpose, spirit and character of the institute which have been ratified by competent ecclesiastical authority as well as wholesome traditions, all of which constitute the patrimony of the institute itself, are to be observed faithfully by all."

The source of this canon is *Perfectae Caritatis*.[9] This canon is important for several reasons, among them being that it requires that religious institutes not only know the legitimate charisms and gifts of the institute and its wholesome traditions, but that they foster and cultivate them. It also suggests that historical changes be distinguished from historical accretions.[10] In paragraph 16:3 of *Ecclesiae sanctae* the emphasis is perhaps made stronger with the mandate given to the religious institutes to strive to recapture the original charism or gift of the institute in the life of the Church. "For the good of the Church, institutes must seek after a genuine understanding of their original spirit, so they will preserve it faithfully when deciding upon adaptations, will purify their religious life from alien elements, and will free it from what is obsolete."[11]

It is clearly seen from these documents, and from the canon that it is incumbent on religious institutes to seek the mind of the founders, if authentic renewal is to take place. Each order and congregation, then, must re-examine its heritage to discover through the founder's writings, actions and early legislation what particular gift the founder brought to the Church.[12] "The best judge of these would be the institute itself, for the effect of such traditions is best seen in how they bear fruit within a community."[13]

Canon 586 makes it imperative that each institute preserve whole and entire its patrimony and that as a result of this each order or congregation enjoy a true autonomy of life, especially an autonomy of governance.[14] In this canon we observe that the Church wishes each religious institute to preserve its legitimate traditions and (the religious institute) safeguard itself from extraneous influences. The basis for this canon can be found in *Ecclesiae Sanctae*, nn. 23, 25, 26, and in the directives of the document *Mutuae relationes* (Congregation of Bishops and Congregation of Religious and Secular Institutes, 14 May 1978). The phrase "true autonomy of life, especially with regard to government" guarantees religious institutes that they are responsible for formulating the directives by which they will be governed, saving the rights of the Holy See. It also reminds the institutes that in matters of governance they are bound to follow the directives of canon 578. This last-mentioned canon is the charter by which the religious institutes are guided in formulating their basic law, and in the manner of regulating their existence through government.[15] The thrust of this canon is to ensure that each institute protects its character and identity, which is special to it, through legislation.

Canon 588 is important because it contains distinctions which many religious institutes find arbitrary and not in accord with the legitimate traditions of their orders or congregations. The first paragraph of the canon states that "the state of consecrated life is neither clerical or lay." This is of the very nature and essence of religious life since all religious are bound by and find their supreme rule of life in the following of Christ as proposed in the Gospel and as expressed in the constitutions of their own institute as canon 662 declares. *Lumen Gentium*, n. 43, speaks of the religious life as a form of life to which some Christians, clerical or lay, are called so that they may enjoy a special gift of grace in the Church. The distinctions made in paragraphs 2 and 3 of canon 588 can be said to be convenient in that they follow some centuries of history and traditional manner of dividing religious institutes. They are not essential or necessary divisions. The institutes may or may not have elements of both states, clerical and lay within their membership.[16]

Many orders, and to a lesser degree congregations, were founded without any distinction between clerical and lay members. One can see from the early history of the monastic and mendicant movements, saving the history of the Dominicans, that these orders were founded on an absolute equality of membership.[17] The governance of monasteries and orders was frequently in the hands of the lay members. Often this was the rule so that priest-members were free to engage in apostolic activities at the service of the Church. It was not uncommon for monasteries, abbeys, friaries, and orders to be governed, with the blessing of the Church, by lay members. It can also be said that these lay members of institutes exercised not only dominative power but true jurisdiction, today called *potestas regiminis* (power of government), over the other members of the community. There is, then, an historical precedent for what so many institutes today ask of the Church, that they be allowed to determine — according to their constitutional law and following the sound traditions of their communities — who shall govern the communities without reference to ordination or non-ordination.

Some institutes have taken issue with the classification of Canon 588 that allows an institute to define itself only as either clerical or lay. The four criteria of Canon 588: intent of the founder, legitimate tradition, supervision by clerics, and the exercise of sacred orders may not all point to the same conclusion. An institute from its beginning may be founded on the basis of equality of members and still have members who exercise orders. It may also be argued that legitimate tradition relates to the intent of the founder more than the fact that for a long period of time priests held most of the offices.

The Society of Mary has used the expression "mixed composition" to explain that there is only one Marianist vocation and that all members have the same rights and duties. Although CRIS requested that the Marianists define themselves as clerical, after some discussion, CRIS accepted the definition that the Marianists were a single family of priests and lay religious. In an article on provincial government in the Marianist Constitutions, it is noted if the Provincial is a priest, the assistant is a lay religious and vice-versa. Thus, together they "reflect the mixed composition of the Society." This arrangement is probably appropriate for a large number of mixed male institutes.

One might argue that in communities now classified as clerical institutes, according to Canon 588.2, only priests may be entrusted with the power of governance. We do see, however, that in another section of the Code of Canon Law, there is provision for lay persons to exercise the power of governance in judicial matters, as in Canon 1421.2. In this case it is a question of participation in the power of governance. The layperson exercises this power in cooperation with those who possess the power by reason of office. In preliminary discussions of the Code Commission, the Secretary informed the sub-commission when discussing paragraphs 2 and 3 of Canon 588 that the Congregation for the Doctrine of the Faith had stated that laypersons could participate in the power of jurisdiction in certain cases when permitted by the supreme authority of the Church.[18] What is most interesting is that this statement gave evidence that the *potestas regiminis* was not intrinsically and inseparably linked with the power of orders as had been the common teaching.[19]

It can be argued from this, as it has been by many orders, that they should be free to nominate from within their membership as superiors those men who are qualified to lead the members in the spirit of the order or congregation, according to the legitimate charisms (gifts) and traditions of the institute. No reference should be made to whether a person possesses ordination or not, since the governance will pertain to the internal ordering and not to the apostolic activity *ad extram*.

The rationale, as proposed by the members of the institutes which seek a change in the discipline of the Church, is that such a change would be sanctioned by Canon 129.2, which states that "Lay members of Christ's faithful can cooperate in the exercise of this same power (*potestas regiminis*) in accordance with the law."

In paragraph one of this canon the power of governance is possessed and exercised by those who receive or have received a sacred order, and who are acting in accord with the prescriptions of the law of the Church. They are capable because they have been ordained.

According to paragraph two of this canon the Christian faithful can participate in the exercise of this power by the norm of the law. The lay person can only cooperate with the person who possesses this power by virtue of holding an office. Thus, the non-ordained Christian faithful would not hold ordinary power, nor could they hold this power vicariously either since such power flows from ordinary power and is joined to a certain office as is explained in Canon 131.

For the exercise of this power, then, it would seem that it is possible for a layperson to be delegated the use of the power of governance. In recent years several indults have been given to religious institutes allowing lay members to act as local superiors, assistant superiors, and in one case a provincial of a mendicant order.[20]   The competent ecclesiastical authority, the Holy See acting through the Congregation of Religious and Secular Institutes, has granted these indults always with the proviso that for any act requiring the use of the power of governance recourse must be had to a priest of the institute. The lay superior becomes an instrument in the flow of governance within the community. He can cooperate with a priest-member in the exercise of governance. In practice the power of jurisdiction that a lay superior could not exercise would relate primarily to the administration of the sacraments, the granting of faculties and dispensations and issuing dimissorial letters. Some of the areas of jurisdiction that would seem to apply to the ordained are:

1. The power to dispense from disciplinary laws in certain cases (Canons 14, 87).
2. The power to dispense from observance of a feast day or a day of penance (Canon 1245).
3. The power to dispense from private vows and oaths (Canons 1196.2° and 1203).
4. To grant dimissorial letters (Canon 1019.1°).
5. To dispense from irregularities and impediments for admission to holy orders (Canon 1047).
6. Faculties for hearing confessions (Canon 969 S2).
7. Permission to establish an oratory (Canon 1223).
8. Faculty to bless a sacred place (Canon 1207).
9. Permission to use a sacred place for another purpose (Canons 1210, 1212, 124 S2).
10. Permission to reserve the Eucharist in an oratory other than the principal oratory of church (Canon 936).

It is clear that most of the authority belonging to a religious superior is not jurisdictional. In addition, the above list is evidence that the most important acts of leadership in a religious community have little to do with jurisdiction. It is possible for an interpretation of Canon 588, coming from the supreme authority of the Church acting in his capacity as legislator, to officially determine which forms of cooperation could be admitted to the lay religious or be denied to them. [21]

The attitude of most religious brothers and most orders and congregations is that religious brothers and religious priests are similar in all ways except for that which flows directly from ordination. Each institute, then, in accordance with its wholesome traditions and the mind of the founder should be able to indicate if it is lay, clerical, mixed. It should also be able to determine the best

possible means for internal self-governance. Orders and congregations are asking if they are not the best judges to discern who is
gifted with the charism of leadership or service from within their
ranks.[22] Members want to be able to choose the person most
suited for leadership without restrictions due to status. The ability
to animate and lead in most cases supersedes the importance of the
power of jurisdiction.

Since all religious of an institute possess a like vocation to
observe the evangelical counsels according to a particular rule or
form of life, they argue that obligations and rights should be equal
for all.

> "A number of theologians are pointing to the important service
> that brothers now provide for focusing on the value, significance
> and nature of religious life, without distinctions between the
> ordained and the non-ordained. Brothers are a special charism and
> vocation of Religious.[23]

> The brothers today recognize themselves as invited to be enablers
> of the laity and promoters of greater collaboration with their bishops
> and the priests and deacons. They are called by vocation to be a
> haven and source of unity, spiritual energy and apostolic vital-
> ity. . . . All the elements in the lifestyle of the brothers are unified
> by their commitment to serve in the spirit of Jesus Christ. The
> constitutive elements or components of their lifestyle are inter-
> related: their faith and zeal; their apostolic spirituality; the fidelity
> that they maintain to a specific charism and tradition; the freedom
> embodied in their vows. . . . We have struggled with our identity
> as religious and equally so as brothers, particularly those in
> so-called 'clerical congregations. . . .' Nonetheless, we are hopeful
> about the future and determined to contribute a uniquely brotherly
> dimension to the life and mission of the Church."[24]

The hope for the future is based on the willingness of Church
leaders to recognize that the call of Vatican II to return to the
original charism of the institute includes allowing the institute to

determine whether they are lay, clerical or neither lay nor clerical. Although this may be an exception to Canon 588 it allows each institute to describe itself as it really is rather than being limited by categories that were neither the intention of the founder nor a legitimate tradition. Even institutes which have a majority of clerics, and have had for many years, do not believe mere numbers make them clerical by legitimate tradition, especially when this was not the intention of the founder. This hope will undoubtedly take the form of many institutes asking the Holy See to recognize them according to their own designation and allowing them to elect leaders without regard to ordination while respecting the canonical authority that is restricted to the ordained.

Endnotes

1 Gaffney, James, F.S.C., "The religious brother in the life of the Church", in *Religious Life in the U.S. Church: the new dialogue* (New York: Paulist, 1984), p. 140.

2 Der, Justin., O.F.M. Cap., *The Capuchin Lay Brother: a juridical-historical study* (Rome: Pontifical University of St. Thomas Aquinas, 1983), pp. 10-11.

3 *Ibid.*, pp. 12-13.

4 *Perfectae caritatis*, n. 8.

5 *Ibid.*, no. 15.

6 Kelly, Thomas C., O.P., "Forward" in *Religious institutes, secular institutes, societies of apostolic life: a handbook on Canons 573-746* (Collegeville: Liturgical Press, 1985), pp. 11-12.

7 *Codex Juris Canonici*, c. 577.

8 Iriarte, Lazaro, *The Franciscan Calling* (Chicago: Franciscan Herald Press, 1974), p. 5.

9 *Perfectae caritatis*, n. 2b.

10 O'Hara, Ellen, C.S.J., "Norms common to all institutes of consecrated life", in *Religious institutes, secular institutes, societies of apostolic life*, p. 36.

11 *Ecclesiae sanctae II*, 16:3.

12 Der, *op. cit.*, p. 237.

13 O'Hara, *op. cit.*, p. 37.

14 *C.I.C.*, c. 586.

15 Der, *op. cit.*, pp. 244-45.

16 *Ibid.*, p. 255: *Lumen gentium*, 43.

17 Sauvage, M., "Fratello", *Dizionario degli istituti di perfezione*, IV (1977), pp. 763-64; Dubois, Jacques, "L'institution monastique des convers," *I laici nella "Societas Christiana" dei secoli XI e XII*, (Milano: Vita e Pensiero, 1968), p. 248; Felder, Hilarin, *Storia degli studi scientifici nell'Ordine Franciscano* (Siena: 1911); Landini, Lawrence, *The causes of the clericalization of the Order of Friars Minor, 1209-1260, in the light of early Franciscan sources* (Chicago: Franciscan Herald Press, 1968), *passim*; Counihan, Cyril, O.S.A., "The brother in clerical religious orders" *Doctrine and Life*, supplement 14 (1976), pp. 29-41.

18 *Communicationes CIC*, (1979), pp. 57-61; Der, *op. cit.*, p. 255.

19 Der, *op. cit.*, pp. 255-57.

20 SCRIS, Prot. no. 9196/83, 4 May 1983.

21 Der, *op. cit.*, pp. 270-74.

22 Gaffney, *op. cit.*, p. 142.

23 *Ibid.*, p. 143.

24 *Ibid.*, pp. 145-46.

II. Experiential Reflections on Cleric-Lay Relationships

A Sisterly Concern

SHEILA CARNEY, R.S.M.
MARGARET CARNEY, O.S.F.

Introduction

W E ARE SISTERS TWICE: sisters by blood and sisters by
religious vocation. We entered different religious congregations, a fact that has resulted in mutual enrichment over the
years. We grew up in the home of our maternal grandmother in a
large working-class parish in Pittsburgh, Pennsylvania. As far
back as we can remember, our extended family included priests.
Some were the pastors and curates of our parish; others were school
chums or relatives; others came into the circle through the charit-
able volunteering done by members of the clan. Like all Catholic
school children of our generation we were subjected to a solemn
catechesis that insisted upon the awesome prerogatives of the
priestly calling. Any distrust concerning the truth of these asser-
tions was dissipated on Report Card Day when we learned existen-
tially just *who* was in charge of our moral and educational formation. Yet these somber experiences which rendered priests distant
and forbidding figures for most of our classmates were cheerfully
balanced at home where we discovered among the members of this

111

fraternity some of our favorite story-tellers, pranksters and child-hood confidants.

This pattern of familial friendship continued when we later moved to a mushrooming suburb whose parish was a bastion of social solidarity for young families of the post-war generation. It continues three decades into the present. The list of clerics, religious brothers and sisters who have come to our parental home to enjoy a fine dinner, a fire on a winter's night, a few hours "away from it all" is a litany full of rich associations. All the members of the family have been the beneficiaries of these bonds. Our most searing griefs, our most boisterous good times have included these persons.

Why do we offer these autobiographical notes? We think that they cast an important light upon the reflections that follow. Part of the blessing and burden of our particular moment in history is the coming of age of women in the life of the Church. While this new historical moment has global manifestations, its impact is most evident in the United States and its subsequent tensions are most obviously affecting the Church in the United States. The forces of social change are not abstract realities, though analysis renders them abstract for purposes of discussion. They are first and last experienced in the lives of individuals as cause and effect. The women's movement which is profoundly altering the life of civic and ecclesial groups is one striking manifestation of the con-temporary search for justice, a justice that reflects biblical values of the Judeo-Christian tradition. Yet it is a movement that finds its roots and bears its results in individual (and often anonymous) lives as well as among the "licensed thinkers" and media-mirrored structures of the age.

As contemporary women we have experienced the two-edged sword that strikes at the false assumptions, the inadquate models of thought and relationship that encumber our times. We are not isolated from the tension. We have suffered both sea-change and soul-change. Yet amidst the swirling current of today's "disputed questions'' and undisputed emotions that they arouse, we continually discover within ourselves a rootedness in the Church. Perhaps it can be most simply stated that we feel ''at home'' in the Church. We state this fully aware of the fact that for many of our contemporaries such a feeling is a relic of the past, a dead memory. We number among our friends — and we know in the wider circle of Church women — those for whom the inequities of unquestioned systems have proven destructive and insupportable. Thus we hasten to add that we are not conjuring a cozy emotional refuge, an idyllic fantasy of the Church as it ought to be. We choose, rather, to be at home in the Church as it is. And, as it is, it struggles with conflict, with sin. Each day we waken to the realization that the Church's messianic potential is most often obscured by the messiness of her incarnational reality. We stand on tiptoe, peering into our lost and locked garden, our darkness lit by the flaming sword.

One of the legends that Pittsburgh has contributed to American folklore is the story of ''Johnny Appleseed.'' Jonathan Chapman saved the seeds from his apple orchard on Grant's Hill. When the first wave of westward pioneering brought folks through the town to the mouth of the Ohio River, Johnny proffered his little packets of seeds as they made their way to the docks. Seeds from a garden of trees. Promise of feathery blossoms in spring. Sturdy fruit in autumn. Our childhood memories, our womanhood's experience yields seeds. These seeds are hope. The hope is that the experience of friendship and discipleship will ultimately transform the categories we call ''cleric'' and ''lay.'' It is the hope of recreating the garden on the frontier that beckons us.

Our reflections are derived from two points of view. First, we wish to briefly examine the problems that we perceive when we observe the internal situation of masculine religious congregations affected by clericalism. We offer observations based on the experience of liturgy, communal celebrations and formation upon which a clerical mentality has an impact. Secondly, we offer reflections upon the manner in which clericalism affects the internal ex-

periences of religious women in their own congregational life and
their external experiences of ministry. We hasten to add that these
observations are precisely that — observations based on experience. They are not an attempt to speak on behalf of religious
women universally, nor do they represent an exhaustive study of
the problem from a feminist perspective.

Having expressed this *caveat*, however, we make a final
introductory point. Religious women do experience clericalism in
very direct and sometimes devasting ways. It is not a subject of
scant interest or importance to us. This is not the place to belabor
explanations that have been done, and done with distinction, in
many other publications. It is in place to note that our reflections
should be read as a kind of reprise of a major theme that demands
the attention and commitment of men and women who are bound
by profession to the life and holiness of the Church.

Observations of Masculine Congregations

INHERITORS of the Judeo-Christian tradition profess religious
beliefs nourished by remembrance. Jews throughout the ages have
been called upon to remember the Passover — Yahweh's great act
of saving love on their behalf — and the covenant which followed
it. The Passover experience freed Jews from the alienation,
marginalization, dehumanization of slavery. The terms of the
covenant called upon them to extend the blessings of inclusion and
dignity to others. The call to inclusivity is heard also by Christian
followers of Jesus whose special care for children, for outcasts, for
the disenfranchised continues to challenge us. Our ability to
celebrate the Eucharist is rooted in our ability to remember, to
re-member. The classic text expressing the Christian summons to
inclusivity is, of course, found in Paul's letter to the Galatians:
''All baptized in Christ, you have all clothed yourselves in Christ,
and there are no more distinctions between Jew and Greek, slave

and free, male and female, but all of you are one in Christ Jesus''
(Gal 3:28, *Jerusalem Bible*). James expressed it even more
strongly: ''Do not try to combine faith in Jesus Christ, our glorified
Lord, with the making of distinctions between classes of people''
(Jm 2:1, *Jerusalem Bible*).

Mutuality

IT IS AGAINST the backdrop of this biblical heritage that the
phenomenon of clericalism, especially when observed within a
particular religious community, is especially jarring. Examples of
the kinds of disjointed relationships produced by clericalism and
the questions raised by them can be found in many facets of
community life — even in something so elemental as how the
members address one another. Within a religious family the
primary relationship is one of brother to brother. In such settings,
the use of one another's given name would seem most natural.
When, however, a particular community relies on the use of titles,
distinguishing between members on the basis of clerical status, it
emphasizes discrimination. All are brothers. Some may be ordained but at the root all are brothers. *Priests for Equality*, in their
pastoral letter, ''Toward a Full and Equal Sharing,'' call upon the
ordained to give up the title ''Father'' because of its patriarchal
overtones. Perhaps religious communities, also striving for a full
and equal sharing among their members, should consider similar
action in their effort to reduce clericalism.

Liturgical Life

STILL ANOTHER DIMENSION of community life where distinctions
between the ordained and the non-ordained may be emphasized is
in the liturgy. In communities where concelebration at Eucharist is

the norm, the ordained vest and gather around the altar while the non-ordained make up the congregation, thus creating a dramatic physical distinction between the two groups. This is especially apparent where recitation of the office precedes Mass. It is a striking experience for the observer to see a community gathered for prayer and then to see it split along clerical lines for the celebration of the Eucharist which is intended to strengthen the bonds of unity among us. It is noted elsewhere in this chapter that, in women's communities, all the preparations necessary to create a prayerful atmosphere in which the Eucharist can be celebrated are done by the sisters "in service of" the priest celebrant. It is interesting to note that in men's communities the non-ordained serve the ordained in these same ways. Perhaps communities would do well to search for ways to allow their liturgical expressions *to more emphatically symbolize unity* rather than distinction.

Educational Equality

PREPARATION FOR ORDINATION and especially the opportunities for theological education afforded by such preparation, may also be points of discrimination. It is assumed that all community members will receive the requisite education for the ministries in which they will serve. What is not assumed is that all will receive equal opportunities for the study of theology and spirituality. Perhaps this is because the theological education which is part of study for ordination is so often viewed as professional preparation rather than part of an ongoing effort to appreciate the full implications of life in Christ. Considered from this latter perspective ongoing theological education is desirable for every community member. An attitude which says we study theology, not only so we can be better homilists or more sensitive administrators of the sacraments, but so that we can all be better brothers, better Christians, is one which helps to eliminate clericalism.

The question of theological education is especially crucial with respect to older non-ordained community members. Communities are encouraged to adopt a stance which expects all members to involve themselves in ongoing theological education as part of their personal formation. But perhaps special sensitivity needs to be expressed for those non-ordained men who entered religious life in the years previous to and immediately surrounding Vatican II. It is assumed that the ordained men of that same vintage have been offered opportunities to update their theology. Can it also be assumed that their non-ordained brothers have been equally encouraged to do so?

In the years since Vatican II, there have been significant changes in the ministerial positions assumed by non-ordained community members. Where they had previously ministered almost exclusively in positions internal to the community, these men now function in a wide range of roles in varied institutions and parish settings. Equality in ministry is becoming an accepted and welcomed facet of life. In communities which sponsor institutions, particularly schools, the ordained and non-ordained function on equal footing as faculty members and administrators alike. Canon Law prevents that same equality from existing in the area of community administration to the extent that the non-ordained are excluded from leadership positions. Communities are challenged to exercise creativity in finding ways to downplay the discrimination engendered by such legislation while "lobbying" at the same time for revisions of canons that promote clericalism.

Another area which calls for creative new approaches is the celebration of jubilees. Clericalism rears its head here in situations where the celebration of ordination anniversaries far outshines the commemoration of religious profession. As in the question of language, the underlying principle is that which gathers these men together primarily is their shared membership in a given religious community. Before all else they are brothers. The call to ordination experienced by some is, indeed, a gift in which to rejoice. But care should be taken to assure that expressions of rejoicing are appropriate and proportionate.

Underlying all these examples of clericalism lies the attitude that to be a priest is to be ontologically "better" than others and that the non-ordained have somehow failed to achieve their real goal. (For why would anyone freely choose not to be ordained?) As long as this insidious attitude persists, whatever efforts are made to eradicate examples of clericalism will fall short and a facade of brotherhood and equality will mask a heart that harbors a sense of superiority and discrimination. In such a heart, the biblical value of inclusivity cannot find a home and the words of James take on an even more challenging tone: "Do not try to combine faith in Jesus Christ, our glorified Lord, with the making of distinctions between classes of people" (Jm 2:1, *Jerusalem Bible*).

Observations from within Feminine Congregations

HAVING OBSERVED THOUGHTS "from the outside" — that is — as women observing the life of congregations of men that are comprised of ordained and lay members, we now turn to a view "from the inside." These reflections highlight some of the tensions that clericalism produces for religious women in two key areas: liturgical life and ministerial relationships. Finally we venture the opinion that religious life is, in its very existence, related to the need in the Church for a variety of ministries that cannot be fully executed and expressed by ordained clerics. This indicates both a vitality in the origins of various types of religious congregations, but it also exhibits some fundamental tensions that arise when religious rise up to meet needs that clerics will not or should not attempt to address.

In the Sanctuary

THE SANCTUARY is the place where, perhaps above all others, the issue of clericalism is symbolically and literally experienced.

Let us acknowledge at the outset the fact that we are not dealing here with a situation in which "anything is possible." Priests and laity alike must, at this point in time, function within structures and regulations (of varying degrees of importance) which govern the nature of our liturgy and seek to transmit the core of our sacred traditions. Yet once we grant this we are immediately confronted with the fact that at present in the Church in the United States the whole area of liturgical celebration as a focus of male-female relationships is more like a mined harbor through which we try to navigate than a family table toward which we turn "in joyful hope." While this is true of the general situation in the Church in North America, it is a problem that is acute in many religious congregations.

Frequent and/or daily participation in the Eucharistic liturgy has long been a core value for countless religious. While this value is often appropriated through participation in a local parish, hundreds of free-standing institutions exist in which the group that celebrates liturgy is exclusively or predominantly composed of religious women or men.

While significant and historic steps were taken in the wake of Vatican II to restore participation of the laity and diversification of liturgical functions, the specific potential of liturgical development within the chapels and oratories of religious communities remains underdeveloped by comparison.

Many if not all religious congregations include persons whose theological and pastoral education equip them for the ministry of preaching. Often the liturgical situation is very specialized in terms of the congregation's charism, spirituality and corporate existence (e.g., religious profession ceremonies, funerals, feasts, anniversaries particular to the congregation, etc.). Frequently liturgy is celebrated as a key element in a larger congregational process or event such as a chapter, discernment period, or special convocation. A priest who is not a participant in the continuing event officiates at the liturgical celebration. In all of these instances — and many not indicated — the current official requirements usually bar a (non-ordained) community member from preaching (cf. Canon 766) and yet the inner unity of the event would be better served by providing for such homiletic service by the religious involved.

Consider further the fact that while women may serve as lectors, minister of music and *extraordinary* Eucharistic minister, the function of acolyte is still technically relegated to males. Sisters who have provided all of the preparatory and correlative liturgical ministries for a solemn celebration may find themselves in the foolish positions of having to forgo acolytes where they would enhance the liturgy rather than be reduced to importing some local grade-school youths where the letter of the law precludes more congruent options.

Beyond the difficulties entailed in actual liturgical celebration looms the entire question of convent chaplaincies. While many priests and sisters can point to inestimable benefits to their personal and ecclesial vocations derived from good experiences of chaplaincy services, countless others can fill more than a few hours with "horror stories" — from both perspectives, no doubt. Chaplaincy assignments usually entail providing suitable living arrangements for a diocesan priest whose work or health makes some other assignment unwise. In spite of the fact that such an assignment involves ministry to a specialized group with its own history, customs, needs and problems, rarely (never!) does the priest thus assigned receive any practical orientation. This can lead to unnecessary error, aggravation and ambivalence that reduce the chances for healthy rapport and effective service. Given the heightened tensions in our contemporary situation it is more important than ever that clergy who minister to and with religious women on a continuing basis be provided with adequate orientation and continuing education services in the hope that they can contribute to the growth of mutuality and play a role in mitigating some of the negative tensions we currently face.

In the Workplace

WHEN DESCRIBING the tensions created by clericalism in working situations we would do well to acknowledge that women religious are not alone in facing this phenomenon. Laypersons are equally involved in the tensions described. Thus, a few factors specific to the interactions of sisters and clergy should be cited.

Unlike many priests and lay co-workers, religious women are acclimated to structures of self-governance and self-determination that give them individually and corporately a high degree of expectation and achievement when it comes to dealing with selection of leaders and the elaboration of common policy. Because of the practice of periodic congregational chapters that elect leaders and determine the directions for their administration, sisters have gained skill and spiritual maturity in handling their internal political processes. This simple fact (established at the price of enormous effort in the last twenty years) means that American sisters probably enjoy twice as much satisfaction relative to a sense of personal access to the systems that govern their lives as their clerical and secular peers. This fact has two important consequences:

a. Sisters enjoy a theoretical and practical knowledge of how to deal with a selection of leaders and policy process.
b. Sisters are able and eager to employ these skills in other Church settings.

What we often discover, however, is that this capability and enthusiasm "fall upon rocky soil." Perhaps it is the instinctive response from many priests that the employment of methods that assume accountability from and rotation of leadership roles are not compatible with a hierarchical system in which authority is achieved by appointment "from above" rather than by election and assent "from below." Rather than deliberately utilizing the learning that has taken place in religious congregations in recent decades, many dioceses and institutions are willing to involve such skills only insofar as basic patterns and attitudes are not challenged, or to superimpose a collegial facade upon an otherwise unconverted monolith.

At the Root

IN SOME WAYS the very existence of large numbers of religious congregations with members in the thousands is a statement about clericalism. As we trace the history of religious life we find that its institutional periods of ebb and flow correlate with the possibilities open to lay men and women for full participation in Church life. In the primitive churches of apostolic times a new egalitarianism flourished. Paul's "neither Gentile nor Jew, male nor female" epitomized this sense of openness and originality. When institutionalization and adoption of secular hierarchical forms of governance took over, women sought alternate roles in monastic and ascetic life forms. Elsie Culver in *Women in the World of Religion* (p. 73) notes that the eventual exclusion of women from hierarchical positions resulted in a great flowering of apostolic activity. The first hospices for pilgrims and hospitals date from this period. Women also exhibited an interest in education and concretized that interest by founding schools. While the charismatic contribution of these "desert mothers," abbesses and mystics enhanced Church spirituality, rarely did women emerge in roles of leadership and authority, save within the feudal monastic realm. Interestingly, when the Gregorian Reform curtailed the power of women within ecclesiastical circles, women turned to the development of new ministries as they had in earlier historical periods. While a radical questioning of this separate but unequal relationship seldom bubbles to the surface of ecclesiatical history, we see in our time a revolutionary shift of consciousness that not only permits the question, but fans it across the popular consciousness of Western Christianity.

A survey of the experience of the exodus from religious life that occurred following the Council shows that among reasons for departures we find the change in awareness that religious life and priesthood were not the exclusive avenues to a life of prayer or ministerial activity. When *Lumen Gentium* strategically placed the universal call to holiness ahead of any consideration of specific religious vocation, the signal was given for a drastic re-evaluation of roles. Members who remained in religious congregations, for their part, were caught up in a massive renovation that also attacked a kind of parallel clericalism among religious women. Both the external trappings that symbolized separation and privilege and the mentality that they revealed were reduced or eradicated. Language changed. Seldom, if ever, does one hear of "the state of perfection," "a higher calling," "Reverend Mother," "when I was in the world." Dress changed. Modes of dress that communicated disdain for and separation from others in the Christian community were modified or abolished. Work changed. Sisters encountered the electronic, technocratic environment and became active in meeting other persons in their own milieu.

In light of this it is hard not to see why particular sensitivity to clericalism exists among sisters who have experienced a liberation within their own ranks from a pyramid model of relationships and from a class consciousness of superiority relative to lay members of the Church. Further, the amount of time dedicated to theological and professional preparation by sisters (an effort that pre-dates the Council) has resulted in the existence of large numbers of women whose general education rivals (and often surpasses) that of the average clergyman. This triad of lived sensitivity, theological insight, and professional equality colors the United States sister's experience and attitudes. They not only find the implied superiority of the clerical outlook abhorrent, but falacious as well.

Conclusion

SINCE WE HAVE OFFERED THESE REFLECTIONS as "sisters" in both senses of the word, we close in that spirit. There have already been a number of efforts among religious and clergy of our country to reconcile some of the tensions described in these pages. Such work is rarely easy, but each effort has value. In the last analysis, however, it appears that each one of us must grapple with the issues "where we are planted." We need not always wait for formal seminars, position papers, or ecclesial or congregational mandates to build the bridges we so urgently need. Perhaps some of the finest work to heal the division that clericalism has inflicted upon men and women has been taken in quiet and unheralded initiatives where brothers and sisters have come together to honestly question, explain, confront and confirm one another. We salute the men and women who in unassuming love have trusted the power of grace and friendship to provide provisional answers and directions amidst our sometimes tangled ways. Such brothers and sisters have believed that the community of the Church is not a lofty ideal to be postponed until the Parousia, but a task that even ordinary folk with ordinary gifts and projects can make present. Let us not be afraid to take such plain and prosaic steps in hopes of finally finding that space and time, when in the words of Julian of Norwich, "all shall be well."

Endnotes

1 Culver, Elsie Thomas, *Women in the World of Religion* (Garden City: Doubleday and Company, Inc., 1967).
2 Priests for Equality, "Toward a Full and Equal Sharing" (West Hyattsville, MD: 1984), lines 800-803.

One Layman's Viewpoint and Vision

PETER GILMOUR

T HERE WAS A POINT in my life when I was so accustomed to calling men who wore cassocks and collars "brother" that when I met a priest I automatically addressed him as "brother." This led to some embarrassment for me, and a variety of responses from the clergy. I did not realize then, but now know thirty years later, that I was touching upon a delicate issue far more complex than a mere slip of the tongue.

I attended Brother Rice High School, Chicago, Illinois from 1956-1960 as a member of the school's charter class. The school was operated by the religious order then known as the Christian Brothers of Ireland (F.S.C.H.), now known as the Congregation of Christian Brothers (C.F.C.). That was the first phase of my life when brothers were influential. I was their student; the brothers were my teachers.

Brothers once again were part of my life after I graduated from college and began teaching high school. I taught at St. George High School, Evanston, Illinois for four years, and after that school closed I continued to teach at another brothers' school, St. Patrick

High School, Chicago, Illinois for five more years. Then for several years after I left high school teaching, I worked with brothers at LaSalle Manor Retreat Center, Plano, Illinois directing retreats for high school students. These two schools and the retreat center were operated by the Brothers of the Christian Schools (F.S.C.). During this phase of my life when I taught high school and then worked at a retreat center, brothers were my colleagues.

The third phase of my life in which brothers have been present is my career as an adjunct professor in the Institute of Pastoral Studies, Loyola University of Chicago. In this graduate program of religious education and pastoral studies, brothers enroll in my courses. Now I am their teacher; brothers are among my students.

As a student of brothers, as a colleague of brothers, and as a teacher of brothers, I am very much aware of the reality and problem of clericalism affecting their lives. As I think about my long and varied association with brothers, several stories, recollections and reflections come to mind which illuminate the reality of and problems with clericalism in the Church.

Brothers as Teachers

I FIRST MET RELIGIOUS BROTHERS when my own brother, who was just fifteen months older than I, entered St. Leo High School, Chicago, Illinois. He would take me along to football and basketball games, school plays, concerts, and other activities. There he would introduce me to some of his teachers. At first, I would mistakenly call them "Father." If they did not correct me, my brother certainly did! And after a while it became routine for me to address these individuals as "Brother."

By the time I entered high school I had become well socialized into the dimension of the local Catholic culture commonly known as "the brothers." My own high school education was unique. I chose not to go to the school my brother attended, but decided to enter a newly opened high school. As freshmen we were the first and only class in the school. Each year for the next three years our class was, in effect, the senior class. Because our class was at first the only class in the school, and also because everything we became involved in was the first — the first football game, the first school newspaper, the first school yearbook — there was a spirit and feeling of accomplishment which, only years later when I began teaching high school, did I realize was unique to my own high school student days.

As I look back on those days now, I realize that the brothers who were assigned to open this new high school were, for the most part, exceptional people who could be depended upon to get this new enterprise off to a good and stable start. Most were young, energetic, personable and demanding teachers. And of course they had their idiosyncrasies which we as high school students noticed immediately. John R. Powers also attended this high school and characterized the more idiosyncratic side of this particular school's life in his novel, *Do Black Patent Leather Shoes Really Reflect Up?*

The priests were in the parish and the brothers were in the school. The clergy were not as involved in our lives as the brothers. For the most part priests seemed older, more distant, and interested in building the parish. From my adolescent perspective, many pastors seemed to be involved in outdoing one another by building bigger, more elaborate churches than their neighboring parishes had constructed. These churches stand today on the southwest side of Chicago as monuments to a bygone era of Catholicism where success was measured in large part by massive amounts of brick and mortar.

I do not recall ever hearing a priest criticize brothers. There was great respect in the Church of my youth for these men. I think this was related to the attitude about and place of Catholic education. For Catholics not to attend a Catholic school was considered more than unacceptable behavior in this very Catholic culture; it was considered sinful. And it was the brothers who conducted a

number of Catholic high schools. Therefore, since Catholic education was not just respected but demanded by faith, the brothers who
delivered this education to so many adolescent children of
Catholics were an integral and respected part of the Church.

Nor do I remember much downgrading of the clergy by
brothers, though they certainly had opportunity and platform for
doing so. Religion classes met daily, and, in addition to the formal
lessons, which in those days were predetermined, fixed and concrete, there still was ample time for discussion. Actually, it took
the form more of question-and-answer periods. Many times during
these sessions students would voice complaints about priests' con-
tinual pleas for money, bad sermons, abrupt confessional style,
and other behaviors. The brothers, who listened to such question-
complaints, seldom took "our" side, but upheld that of the priests.

Looking back on my high school years from today's perspective, I realize it was largely the model of Church taught and the
approach to sanctity advanced which put priests over brothers, and,
indeed, over everyone else. This both fostered and re-inforced
clericalism. The triangular/hierarchical model of Church put pope,
bishops and priests near the top, brothers and sisters closely following (but still distinctly below), and, at the base, lay people. Toward
the top of the triangle, ministers (this word would not have been
used at that time) had their place, and those people who were
ministered to had their place towards the bottom of the triangle.
Those people at the top of the triangle were ministry producers;
those people at the bottom of the triangle were ministry consumers.
This model of the Church was neat, orderly and considered worthy
of acceptance during that period.

The approach to sanctity was intimately related to this
triangular/hierarchical model of Church. The higher up the triangle
a person's chosen state in life, the higher the calling, and, by
association, the more assured of sanctity one became. Even though
this corporate structure of spirituality was theoretically balanced by
the concept that each person was called to a particular state in life

— and one needed not only to find out but also to become what he/she was called to — there was great emphasis placed on the desirability of answering and achieving a "higher calling."

Is it any wonder that with such a model of Church and vision of sanctity tensions should arise between brothers and priests? The contemporary Church has come to realize this triangular/ hierarchical model is a flawed understanding of Church and produces an inadequate vision of sanctity. The understanding of the Church as the People of God, the call of all Christians to holiness, and the understanding of ministry as both a right and an obligation of all Christians, all of which have been voiced since the Second Vatican Council, reflects a radically different understanding of Church and produces a radically different vision of sanctity.

And so the brothers of my youth, loyal to the vision of Church and approach to sanctity then being taught, and probably sublimating what their own life experiences were able to teach them, dutifully instructed their students in this triangular/hierarchical vision of Church and approach to sanctity. No one really thought to challenge this model of Church except through the one perennial question of our incredibly immature minds housed in our wildly adolescent bodies: How can brothers, or anyone else for that matter, possibly opt for chastity? The brothers therefore were accessories before, during and after the fact; they supported a model of Church and an approach to sanctity which fostered clericalism. So too did the whole Church. It simply believed and taught.

Brothers as Colleagues

AFTER GRADUATING from high school, I began teaching at a Catholic high school operated by brothers. It was there that I realized more fully that brothers had a distinct identity vastly different from priests, and they wanted to make sure that it was clearly understood as such. They wanted no part of clericalism, which was associated with priests. I remember one incident quite well. In 1966 there was an open-housing march in the community where the school was located. The brother principal invited the faculty to join him in the march. I joined him, and the stepping off place was a local Protestant church. There, after a prayer service, the march to the city hall was about to begin. The organizers of the march asked the clergy to come to the front and to lead the march. My brother principal did not move. I later asked him why he did not move to the front of the march, and he said to me, "That would have violated what I believe. I am not a clergyman, nor do I want to be recognized as one." It was an eye-opening remark for me because I, like so many other people, had unconsciously grouped all religious, whether they be priests, sisters or brothers, together as one entity.

I taught for this religious order of brothers for nine years, and worked with them at a retreat center for several more years. Time and time again I felt this attitude I first learned on that open-housing march was a tradition with the brothers. They had their own identity not at all associated with the clergy. And therefore as a group they did not want to be associated with or to manifest clericalism, i.e., having or taking privileges because of their place near the top of the hierarchical triangle. They were themselves hard working professional educators contributing their talents to the Church and to society. They possessed an identity needing neither ordination to function effectively in their chosen ministry nor artificial prestige at the expense of other groups within the Church.

It was during these years I spent working with brothers at the LaSalle Manor Retreat Center, Plano, Illinois that I became aware of yet another area of tension that sometimes exists between priests and brothers, and this centered around the celebration of Reconciliation and Eucharist during retreats. There was no priest on the staff of the retreat center, and therefore priests were "brought in" to preside at Reconciliation and Eucharist.

Many of these priests were men who could easily fit into the dynamics of the retreat, and they were effective presiders at Reconciliation and Eucharist. Of course, a few were not attuned to adolescents, the retreat program, or new understandings of Church and community. Such priests were inflexible about how Reconciliation and Eucharist could be celebrated, and therefore were not open to adaptation for the particular and unique circumstance of a retreat experience for adolescents.

The student retreatants were not particularly hostile to these men and their style of sacramental celebration; rather, such sacramental celebration became irrelevant for the student retreatants. And so the most cherished and treasured parts of our religious heritage became irrelevant because of a form of clericalism. How could the retreat staff — both brothers and lay people alike — be anything but disappointed in such an experience?

But a deeper issue eventually surfaced for the retreat house staff. That issue centered on who *best* presides at the celebration of sacraments for a specific community of faith. Even those priests who could fit easily into this unique situation still were outsiders to the retreat community. They functioned as presiders of these specific assemblies because of the office they held in the institutional Church, not because of the role they played in these particular local communities of faith.

The retreat staff saw each successful retreat group become a specific and unique Christian community, and we realized that *community* is the primary sacrament. This is the sacrament from which all other sacraments emerge. Therefore the practice of bringing in an outside priest, good and effective though he may have been, violated this understanding of sacramentality, and reinforced an institutional type of clericalism which is more a vestigial organ in the new Church than a requirement for validity of the sacramental process. [1]

I am not suggesting that tensions between brothers and priests would best be solved by the ordination of brothers. Not at all. I am suggesting that one of the root causes of clericalism in the Church today is the detachment of ordination, and therefore priesthood, from local communities of believers. Ordination is usually seen as a "top-down" sacrament whereby the institution bestows priesthood upon select members. Since I see *community* as the primary sacrament from which all other sacraments, including ordination, emerge, conferring priesthood should be a "bottom-up" sacrament whereby select members emerge from the communities of faithful for service to these communities. If the Church could regain the intimate link between priesthood and community in practice, then, I believe, clericalism would vastly diminish.

As I reflect upon today's Church and what the future Church might be, I am struck with how "clericalism" is still present, but no longer solely among the clergy. It can be found in all areas of ministry — lay people, sisters, brothers, priests and deacons. And likewise clericalism's opposite, which I believe to be an authentic ministry of service, is also present across the spectrum of rank and position. Therefore priests, brothers, sisters, lay people and deacons possessing a true ministry of service orientation have far more in common with each other than those of their own group oriented towards clericalism. Just as the Church is experiencing a proliferation of ministries, so too is it experiencing a proliferation of clericalism. One has only to witness the emergence of clericalism in the permanent diaconate to see an all too apparent example. And wherever this attitude manifests itself, be it in pope, peasant, or priest, it is not good for the Christian community.

Brothers as Students

THE MOST RECENT PHASE of my life with brothers is my role as a teacher of brothers who study in the Institute of Pastoral Studies at Loyola University of Chicago. People from the entire English-speaking world come to study in this program; among this student body are many brothers. They are professionally oriented, interesting people, concerned not only about the students they teach and/or the work they do, but also about the world in which they live.

One of the major attitudinal differences I have observed between priests and brothers deals with their own continuing education. As a group brothers are much more oriented to continuing their own education. Diocesan priests by and large do not have this same desire or interest in education. I observe this in the number of priests as compared to the number of brothers in our program. An exception is priests from religious orders, who generally are much more open to continuing education than are diocesan priests.

There is a story, perhaps apocryphal, that a now deceased controversial bishop of a large archdiocese, when presented with an ambitious in-depth plan for the continuing education of clergy remarked, "Isn't my ordination good enough for them?" By contrast, I have found that mostly all the leadership of brothers' orders have a positive attitude toward continuing education for their members, and have spent a good deal of time and money encouraging members to further their own education, regardless of their stage of life or of how many previous degrees they might have earned.

There is another dimension which concerns me as I look to the future of the Church, the local Christian communities and the religious orders of brothers. This dimension concerns the reality of a continuing decline in the numbers of brothers in comparison to the needs of the ministries for which they are currently responsible. I return specifically to reflect on the Catholic school as an example. It is common today for religious orders of brothers to operate schools in which they themselves are the vast minority of the faculty, sometimes as low as five or ten percent. So what exactly is their role in schools and other ministerial settings where brothers find themselves in the minority?

Some orders of brothers have collectively decided that their role should be to occupy positions of leadership and influence within their institutions. Might this not be a form of ecclesiastical apartheid where the minority has access to roles denied the majority? This is certainly a form of clericalism where office rather than competence determines who is eligible for certain positions, for example, principal, chairperson of the religion department, director of guidance and counseling, and so on.

Most brothers I have met these past years at the Institute of Pastoral Studies want to be judged by their competence, not by their office. I find this refreshing and encouraging. Yet I know many lay people who work alongside brothers in mutual ministerial settings, and these lay people are not yet eligible to serve in some positions because they are not brothers.

I have led an interesting and interacting life with brothers. They were my teachers when I went to high school; I became their colleague for more than a decade when I taught high school and directed youth retreats; and, now, I am teaching brothers in a graduate school program. Thus, these reflections, personal and experience-based, flow from this long and interesting association with brothers.

It has been many years since I have mistakenly called a priest, "brother," that strange habit of my youth. The reason is not an improved memory for formal titles. Rather I now honor these men by using their baptismal names. By doing so I avoid the traps and trappings of clericalism while at the time I affirm their vocational call to ministry which flows from baptism. Thus, by emphasizing baptismal heritage rather than secondary roles and titles, I am hopefully imaging a Church of the future in which we all are invited to participate as adult equals.

Endnotes

1 I have explained the relationship between community, sacrament and priesthood in *The Emerging Pastor* (Kansas City: Sheed and Ward) 1986.

The Continuing Struggle of a Mixed Community

PATRICK HANSON, C.P.

I T WOULD BE DIFFICULT to speak of my experience of clericalism in men's religious communities without relating to my own community. I do want to say at the outset that my community has taken some very positive steps in dealing with the issue of clericalism and continues to struggle with it.

I entered the community after graduating from college. At that time I was twenty-four years old and the first college graduate interested in being a religious brother in my province. The role of the brother was beginning to undergo great changes and I was told to be patient. The brother's ministry was confined to the in-house tasks such as cooking, tailoring and maintenance. In terms of the brother's legal standing in the community, he had neither active nor passive voice in the local community, nor on the provincial or congregational level. Many, I think, would have described the brother's ministry at this time as one of support for the priest's ministry.

As a postulant I persevered for about six months, being assigned to learn the tailoring of religious habits, cooking, and worst of all, I thought, spending a day each week doing the community laundry. While I worked in the laundry the cleric novices, most of whom had just graduated from high school, were allowed to recreate or study. The system certainly had something to do with my leaving the community, but the deeper issues were those of call. I really was not ready.

An awareness of clericalism and what that meant was not part of my consciousness at that time. There were things about the system that did not seem right. I remember being cornered by a couple of priests and asked why I did not want to study for the priesthood since I was a college graduate. Through much of this, my attention was focused on the romantic notion of monasticism and of being a monk.

In Webster's Collegiate Dictionary, clericalism is defined as ". . . maintaining or increasing the power of the religious hierarchy." My experience has not been so much the problem of the increase of clerical power as the refusal to let it go. The frustration of this system then was the question of how to contribute input into a system that is controlled by the ordained, who hold the power.

Upon leaving the community I enrolled in graduate school and received a Masters in Secondary Education. During this time the thought of being a religious brother was continually with me, so upon graduating I did return to the community. Much of the old novitiate system had changed in the two years I was gone. Now the chores of the house were shared by all the novices and the discussion of my teaching after novitiate would become a reality.

The tension in religious life between the cleric and the brother is not something of recent times. In 1185 in the Order of Grandmont, the brothers claimed equal rights in the monastery and when refused they expelled the prior and two hundred choir monks. In 1219 they again deposed the prior and forty choir monks. In light of this the response of brothers in more contemporary times has been quite meek.[1]

Stories are fairly common of founders who were coerced into ordination, or at least strongly encouraged, in order to have their rules accepted. In 1985 the Franciscans at their General chapter elected a brother to the council. Even though Francis himself was never ordained, the brother elected in 1985 was the first brother on a council in seven hundred and fifty years.

The 1986 Kennedy Catholic Directory lists a total of 7,429 brothers and 57,183 priests (22,028 being religious priests) in the United States. As one begins to subtract the retired and infirm brothers and those brothers living in more cloistered situations, very few brothers are left present to the Church in terms of role models. The small number of brothers, the lack of understanding of the brother's call, and its comparison to priesthood as the norm present obvious implications in terms of brother vocations.

All brothers are familiar with statements such as, "Why don't you go all the way?", or "You are so good you should be ordained." These statements come from all segments of the Church whether lay, religious or ordained. In working with one of our brother candidates who was employed in a Catholic hospital, I once asked him if he told the people at the hospital that he was a candidate for our community. His response was that he did when he first started the job, but finally stopped telling anyone because when he did they always responded by asking him, "Why not a priest?" It would have been a good opportunity to educate people, but being unsure of the call to brotherhood himself, he was in no position to defend it.

Because of the lack of understanding of the brothers' vocation exhibited by many segments of the Church there is little support for those discerning the call. This is particularly true in the mixed communities where candidates tend either to choose ordination or to opt out completely. In years past it was easy to decide who would be the brother, as there was little formal training required. Today's candidates interested in being a brother are coming to religious life with a college degree but with little knowledge of the call. Many are still confronted with the question, "Why not a priest?"

In my six years of vocation ministry for my community and also for a large diocese, I experienced the lack of understanding of who a brother is in the Church. As a vocation director I learned to dread, in most cases, a candidate sent to me by a diocesan priest or a sister. The person usually was not acceptable for the priesthood and with his limited abilities and gifts could not, I felt, be a brother either.

With the growing shortage of candidates for the priesthood, I believe the pressure to ordain men interested in brotherhood will continue to increase. A brother candidate who is intelligent and talented and who has a good personality will probably encounter subtle humor about choosing priesthood and will not sense much support for the call to brotherhood. Sometimes the lack of support in community, whether conscious or not, is not as negative as the lack of understanding from family, friends and those encountered in ministry. In the minds of many people there always seems to be an element of choosing "second best".

One might raise the question as to whether it is possible for the cleric and lay religious to live together, or if it is even desirable. One of my "wisdom" figures in community told me once that he felt that if priests and brothers cannot live together in community, then how can we expect our lay brothers and sisters in the Church to live with their ordained brothers in a spirit of Christian community.

There certainly is a richness in a both lay and cleric community that is not present in communities that have only one or the other. For myself, the possibility of having one of my brothers who is ordained celebrate Eucharist with me is a gift. I recognized this even more after talking with one of my religious sisters concerning the fact that women religious always have to bring someone in from outside to celebrate Eucharist for them. The complementarity of gifts, whether personal or the result of a particular vocational call, cannot help but enrich the local community and the Church as a whole when all are treasured and encouraged for who they are.

Even though individual brothers have found new ministries and are developing a new image of the brother for themselves, there is still minimal movement in the corporate image of brother. The small number of brothers, the lack of professional training for many, and a role that has been affirmed over the years as not being assertive, has meant that input from the brother members of the community has been minimal.

Some provinces in a number of congregations no longer have brothers, and some have, for all practical purposes, decided no longer to admit brother candidates. I know of one community where a province decided to drop the word brother from their title, as there were no brothers in the province and they had decided not to recruit any. Thank God the rest of the congregation did not find their decision acceptable. I know there is no easy solution to this problem, but I am personally convinced that a congregation that allows the brother's vocation to die when it was a part of the founder's vision is not being faithful to that vision.

With few brothers around to serve as role models, the acquiring of an identity as a brother can be a problem. Some brothers will adopt the dress of a priest and then wonder why everyone calls them ''Father.'' Other brothers may identify so much with their particular profession that one has no idea that they are religious. Somewhere in between there has to be an identity that clearly speaks of a lay religious commitment.

I remember very distinctly the various stages I have gone through in trying to establish my own identity as a brother and to articulate a positive definition of what I am about in the Church. The first stage in terms of definition was the negative stage; what I am not. I usually started by saying I am *not* ordained and I do *not* hear confessions. After a while I felt that I was being apologetic about my role in the Church. The next step was a definition that played off of the role of the sister in the Church. I would say, ''I am

like a sister . . .," knowing that most people could relate to this
analogy. My final stage came while attending a vocation meeting. I
heard a brother divide the vocation of the religious brother into two
categories: that of ministry and that of lifestyle. In terms of a
brother's ministry, there is nothing he can do in the Church that is
not open to his lay sister and brother. What differentiates a
brother's call is that he lives in a community and has chosen to live
the vows.

Gaining this insight was a significant event in defining for
myself my own presence in the Church and community. This
meant that I shared the fraternity and the charism of our founder
with my brother priests, but that I found my identity in ministry
with my lay brothers and sisters.

Not only was I able to formulate a definition for myself, but it
also helped me decide what I would wear while I ministered. At
one point when I was teaching I wore a so-called Christian
Brother's collar. Working in the environment of a brother's school,
it automatically identified me as a brother. Whenever I wore the
brother's collar and went beyond the boundaries of the school and
into the broader Church, however, people would automatically
assume I was a priest. Many times now when I am present in a
ministerial or social situation with some of the ordained members
of my community, people assume I am a priest. This is due to the
fact that all of our public ministry in the past was through the priest,
so that people are totally unaware that the community had religious
brothers. After about ten years of profession and having gone back
and forth between a collar and a tie and coat, I finally settled on the
latter. If in my ministry I identify myself with my lay brothers and
sisters, I want to be consistent then in terms of my visible identity.

Another significant issue for me is that I want people to go
away remembering me as a brother. Because we are so few it is
very important that people know who we are. When I wear a tie and
coat people do not assume that I am a priest, and as a result are open
to hear the word "brother."

In my own community and in others during the renewal years after Vatican II the question was often raised as to how the brothers fit into a religious community that had both brothers and priests. Workshops were held and papers were written trying to justify the brothers' presence. I have always felt that we were asked the wrong question, and I think the recent findings of the Vatican Study of Religious Life in the United States, especially in terms of vocations, support this: "In fact, religious superiors frequently note that religious clergy often seem to have a stronger identity as priests than as religious." From my own experience in community I have always found many of the tensions between community and ministry do revolve around priesthood and how it fits into religious life. I am encouraged that the Conference of Major Superiors of Men is pursuing this issue to assess religious brotherhood and priesthood in the context of community.

Related to this is the fact that a brother cannot continue to minister in the Church as brother if he decides that he does not want to live in community. Priests on the other hand have the option of leaving community life and of being incardinated in a diocese. I am not advocating this possibility for brothers, but it does at times affect the commitment of religious priests to a community.

The formation of brother candidates in a mixed community has always been a problem and continues to be so in most communities. Much of the problem has to do with the lack of candidates and the question of what the brother's role is in the Church. Is he still a priest's helper, or does he have a role of his own? In searching for answers to the formation problem we have many times fit the brother into the clerical model of training. We have done this because it is the only model we have and also because brothers in their struggle for equality have bought into this model. The problem with this, as I see it, is that in some instances we are producing junior clerics and not lay ministers. I am definitely not speaking against theological and scriptural studies, but I think the nature of the studies and at times the actual school in which the studies take place have to be flexible and adaptable to the various needs of the individual brother.

My own community comes out of a tradition in which the brothers were in a sense the backbone of community life. My concern is that in our striving to become more professional ministers in the Church, we are paying a price in terms of our commitment and presence to one another in community. Brothers today need not only to be professionally trained to minister to the broader Church, but to have access to the spirit present in our older brothers that made home a pleasant place to return to.

Another problem I see in some communities is the situation in which the taking of final vows, normally incorporating one as a full member of the community, has very little meaning as measured against the clerical member's ordination. We have to develop tangible signs that say final vows are in themselves important and do make a difference. Without this, priesthood is still the focus and continues to determine full membership. One way of having a great effect on strengthening the bonds of fraternity in community is the brothers' coming to some awareness that they also have "power" and possess the charism of the founder. In some communities where the vocation of the brother is dying out there is no great panic. Yet, if one were to suggest that there would be no more priests in such a community, many would feel the community could no longer exist, even if brothers were still present. The sad point is that many brothers would also think the community is dead.

Somehow our brothers in training have not taken ownership for themselves of the community's charism. I mean this in the sense that some believe there has to be a priest present to validate the charism. In those communities or provinces where there are no longer any brothers, one seldom hears a conversation as to whether the community is dying. On the other hand it would be inconceivable for many, including brothers, to believe they could go on without priests present.

A few years ago one of my brother priests and myself proposed to the provincial council that a candidate house be established specifically for brother candidates. We saw as the purpose of this house to affirm and support those candidates discerning the brothers' vocation so that they would hopefully survive as they moved along in the system.

In one sense it would have been good if this house were staffed only by brothers so that the brothers and the rest of the province could see that the charism could survive. We did not choose to go this way, which in the long run is best as it shows the importance of a mixed lay/clerical presence in our communities.

A major source of disunity in mixed communities today is Rome's insistence that as a norm only priests can serve as the major superior of a community. A few years after taking final vows I was elected local superior of the community I was living in and the election was rejected because I was a brother. As a community we did play along with the "game" by dropping the canonical status of the house; I was then named the coordinator. Today a brother can be a local superior.

The bottom line in all of this for me is the vocational issue. How can I tell a man interested in our community, one who is well educated and has a positive sense of self, that we are all equal in community, brothers and priests, but that he can never be the major superior of the community? It is issues like this that cause those interested in being a brother to choose priesthood or to leave.

In 1982 the Union of Superiors' General had a series of meetings on the religious brother and issued a report. The results of the study were largely dismal and are summed up in four points:

1) some brothers are becoming priests;
2) some brothers are leaving religious life because they are frustrated;
3) some brothers and priests are dissuading candidates from remaining brothers;

4) some older brothers are struggling desperately to maintain the old system, which is leaking on all sides.

Personally, I can say that I have witnessed all four symptoms in the United States.[2]

As a result of these findings Pope John Paul II called for a special plenaria on the "Mission and Ministry of Brothers in Clerical and Lay Communities." However, the permanent members of the plenaria were all ordained. No brother sat as part of the plenaria. The National Assembly of Religious Brothers and the Conference of Major Superiors of Men exerted strong efforts to convey input to the plenaria, and Bishop Anthony Bevilacqua (then bishop of Pittsburgh) a member of the plenaria, met with influential brothers before going to Rome. But it was disconcerting that in the end one of the participants in the plenaria was quoted in a press release saying, ". . . jurisdiction is reserved by Divine law to clerics."[3]

It is my perception that brothers in mixed communities have a deep sense of the lack of support for their vocation. Much of their ministry takes place either in one of their community ministries, where they are the minority, or in the broader Church where they are alone. They are not in the environment of a teaching brother who is in an institution that is often owned by brothers and identified solely with brothers. I have seen brothers from mixed communities respond to those in ministry who presume them to be priests by either getting angry, by trying to educate the person about a brother's call, or more often out of frustration by letting people assume they are priests.

Some communities of brothers, in my experience, can themselves be very clerical, and this is expressed through clerical dress and a certain aloofness from the local Church. Some have bought into the status quo and have allied themselves completely with the hierarchical Church rather than exercise their prophetic stance as many of their religious sisters have. The brothers' communities have a greater freedom to respond to various Church issues, like their religious sisters, because they are not ordained ministers over whom the hierarchy can exercise some control by threat of the withdrawal of faculties.

I believe that religious sisters and brothers should collaborate much more, not only for the good of the Church but also because they both have responded to the same call. I believe the sisters need the support and presence of men as brothers need the presence and support of women. Both groups are oppressed in some way and need to share this reality so we can move forward positively together.

As with many minorities, the brothers themselves suffer from infighting that tends to take energy away from positive growth. There can be divisions between the younger and older brothers, between those doing in-house ministry and those involved outside, or between brothers in mixed communities and those from all brothers' communities. We have to recall one another to the deeper fact that we have all responded to the same call.

At present the prognosis for the brother in the Church looks rather grim, especially in the mixed communities. With the continuing shortage of priests I believe the pressure will increase to ordain all men interested in ministry in the Church.

My greatest sadness in seventeen years of professed life was to hear a brother whom I admire very much say that if he had it to do all over again, he would have joined a community of brothers. He is not saying he does not feel at home in the community or that he does not share in its charism, but rather he questions the amount of energy it has taken to survive as a brother. This energy could have been put to much better use in ministry. I have seen other brothers over the years grow tired of the struggle and leave, but most have settled into a ministry and in a sense have faded into the background feeling they have contributed as much as they can to the continuing struggle. It is that struggle which challenges me.

Endnotes

1 Br. Edward Cashin, F.M.S., "History of the Lay Character of the Religious Brother Vocation", *Brother*, p. 10, 1968.
2 Report: Union of Superiors General "Conventus Mensilis," February 10-12, p. 5, 1982.
3 News Release, Vatican City, January 24, 1986.

Being Forgotten and Forgetful:
A Subtle Clericalism

BR. MICHAEL McGINNISS, F.S.C.

One Point of View

A FUNDAMENTAL AXIOM of the criticism of novels and short stories is to determine the point of view from which the story is told. A similar axiom should probably apply to this narrative of experiences with the phenomenon of clericalism in the Roman Catholic Church. Not only does the writer's viewpoint determine what he has experienced, but it also affects the way he interprets the very experiences which form the narrative. Of course in real fiction the story teller will often reveal the standpoint unconsciously in the telling of the tale. In this kind of writing, an attempt to be more straightforward and self-conscious is called for at the outset.

I have been a member of the Brothers of the Christian Schools, sometimes known as the De La Salle Brothers, since 1965. The Christian Brothers, as we are popularly known, have been a completely brothers' order since the days of our founder, St. John Baptist De La Salle, himself the first and only priest in the order. In the United States, our order is involved almost exclusively in educational works, chiefly in schools administered by some of the brothers. In my own province or district, which encompasses Pennsylvania, Maryland, and New Jersey, brothers can remember times not too long past in which the brothers constituted 75% and higher of the faculty of our schools. In fact when the brothers staffed their first high school in Philadelphia, the agreement with the archdiocese stipulated a faculty composed totally of brothers. Today, the number of brothers in any school is but a fraction of the total faculty.

I mention the issue of the composition of our faculties since it illustrates that my fellow Christian Brothers have tended to work in settings in which they could be in control. As a matter of fact, in situations where we were teaching in schools under the administration of a priest, usually a diocesan priest, we found the situation unsatisfactory and typically withdrew from the school. Thus, the usual professional situation in which Christian Brothers find themselves is one in which they are in control and do not have to interact with priests in a direct day-to-day way. This is not to say that the Christian Brothers are, or ever have been, totally insulated from clericalism, but rather that such experiences are not at the heart of either our apostolic-professional or community lives.

In addition, I am a professor of theology and religion at a university sponsored and still administered largely by Christian Brothers. My theological training, at the University of Notre Dame, involved a significant amount of research into the experience of parish members and groups of people at the grass-roots of the Church. As a result, I try to look at the life of the Church from the bottom up by concentrating on the experiences of the people in the pews rather than on the experiences of leadership personnel. This theological lens, if you will, accounts in part for the approach in the following narrative and especially in the vignette dealing with the seaside pastor.

As Christian Brother I have encountered almost nothing of that form of clericalism which sometimes characterizes the experiences of brothers in communities with both priest and brother members, the so-called mixed communities. When I have been with brothers from these communities and been able to listen to some of their stories, I have come away wondering why they remain in situations within which they often confront indignities and condescension. Particularly vivid in my memory is a retreat I attended while studying for my doctorate in theology at Notre Dame. The retreat was held at a popular retreat center in the upper Midwest. The participants represented a broad cross-section of brother's orders. Over the three days of the retreat, brothers from mixed communities related many stories of having to cater to priests in their communities. For some, the tensions provoked by the priests' expectations amounted to nothing less than a crisis of conscience. And it was that dimension of their experiences which made it difficult for me to understand and appreciate their patience and perseverance in the community. One particularly poignant incident from that retreat stands out in my memory: a conversation with a so-called "working brother" from a mixed community. He was agonizing over just how much he was required to serve the needs and whims of the priests, even to the point of dipping their ice cream after dinner.

Having said that I personally experience few if any of those obviously pernicious effects of clericalism does not make them any the less significant. In fact, the present climate within the Church seems to be aggravating differences between priests and brothers in mixed communities. Recently some mixed communities have changed their constitutions to permit brothers to serve as local, regional or even general superiors, but finds Rome insisting that only priests can serve in such capacities. In addition, the fact that any such differences still exist indicates that there is much to be done in terms of integrating the egalitarian principles of Vatican II into the internal life of many religious orders, as well as into the daily experience of many Roman Catholics.

Rather than musing about experiences which I have not had, I will focus on a dynamic that derives from clericalism and which is a very subtle, yet intrusive, aspect of Church life. That dynamic is one of "being forgotten and forgetting" and it applies to the brothers in my order as well as to men and women in the Church generally, whatever their vocational choice. Being forgotten will seem a familiar experience to brothers, who frequently hear people list the celibate vocations in the Church as "priests and sisters" and omit the brothers. The forgetting that I have in mind is forgetting the charisms of baptism, the ordination that all members of the Church have received which commits them to the challenge and responsibilities of Christian witness in the world. While this dynamic of "being forgotten and forgetting" is often not a dramatic experience, it forms for me, as I believe it does for many other brothers, one of the dominant experiences of clericalism. The net result of this dynamic affects everyone in the Church by masking the effects of clericalism, almost blinding everyone — sisters, brothers, priests and lay women and men — to the existence and persistence of clericalism.

Being Forgotten: Why We Didn't Go "All the Way." or The Brother: Forgotten and Forgetful!

AN OBVIOUS BEGINNING for an essay like this is the kind of experience with which most religious brothers are familiar: answering the question why we didn't "go all the way" and become priests! Lay persons and priests ask this question of us and, in so doing reveal the presence of a clerical bias in the mind of much of the body politic of Roman Catholic Church. Such questions are especially frustrating when posed by women and men who we think should know better, often our very own families and friends. However, precisely by being so obvious, these questions are the least illuminating place to begin. For as frustrating as such experiences are, they are only the tip of the iceberg in this dynamic of being forgotten and forgetting.

An undramatic, even innocent, experience captures this aspect of clericalism: my being in the audience for an address on the state of ministry given by a noted woman theologian. The context for the address was a university campus in the midst of a summer session of graduate education for women and men interested in preparing for careers of ministry or in updating themselves in the midst of very busy such careers. Many of those present were religious brothers, a high percentage were members of my own order. As one would expect, much of the speaker's presentation concentrated on problems in ministry deriving from inequalities among women and men. She cited numerous examples — always identifying the kinds of roles which the people in her examples had in the Church. Never once in the course of the talk, which lasted close to an hour, did she mention religious brothers, either as a positive or negative factor in the general picture she painted for the audience.

When I asked the speaker about this exclusion, she was momentarily taken aback — largely because she had been unaware of making it. After some consideration, she replied that her own view of brothers is that generally they are not on the side of clerics and thus not quite as much part of the problem created by clericalism. Still, her silence on the matter spoke volumes about her unconscious perceptions and her lived experience of the ways that brothers typically have not impacted on the structures of the Church, especially here in the United States.

Another incident reveals the second half of the title of this section: that brothers are ''forgetful'' members of the Church. For five years after leaving graduate school, I taught on the faculty of a Roman Catholic graduate school for theology and ministry. There much of the student's conversation dealt with the pros and cons of ordaining women. Women students typically supported ordaining women and feminist causes generally. Among the men, who were usually candidates for ordination in a religious order, opinion was divided with some in favor of ordaining and others tending to be opposed, though often quietly for fear of becoming a *cause célebre*. In some conversation about this matter, I observed that simply ordaining women into the present structures for ministry might not necessarily achieve great changes within Roman Catholicism. One woman student reminded me that I felt that way because I had had the opportunity to be ordained, being a man, but had chosen not to pursue that career. Women, on the other hand, can never make that choice, being perpetually excluded in the basis of their sex.

In effect because of being men and because of the still dominant maleness of the Church, religious brothers find themselves separated by their gender from the experiences and the sufferings of religious women and those who are seeking to diversify the ministered life of the Church. As a consequence, religious brotherhood is often set apart from the kinds of situations and struggles which confront many people in the Church. Experiencing this aspect of clericalism does not have anything to do with conscious choice on the part of the brothers. There is a certain determined quality about this experience: we are men and that is unavoidable. Maleness, however, insulates us from some of the very experiences that are presently so divisive in the Church. Probably most brothers are sympathetic to the various excluded groups within the body of the Church. And while we are certainly sympathetic and even equipped to be more than sympathetic largely because of our own unique role as "forgotten persons," we are often forgotten and not involved. This same forgetfulness has contributed, in part, to the "forgetting" manifested by the theologian described in the earlier incident.

As a Christian Brother, this dual experience of being "forgotten and forgetful" is neither completely painful nor destructive. Certainly, unlike our colleagues in mixed groups with priests and brothers, we do not have to confront compromises with our sense of self-worth and self-confidence in order to co-exist side by side with clerics. Being ''forgotten'' by the Church establishment is not a particularly harmful experience for me or my colleague Christian Brothers because we are recognized and respected in education, which is the primary apostolic focus of our order. Nor is the experience of being ''forgotten'' completely without its benefits in the ominously authoritarian climate which pervades the relationship between the Vatican and US Catholics today. Not that brothers totally escape the notice of the Church's authorities, but by and large they are more invisible when Roman heresy hunters survey the landscape (somewhat ironic in that many Christian Brothers are actively involved in religious education and thus participate in the teaching ministry of the Church).

But the principal criterion by which to judge these experiences of being forgotten and forgetting is not the amount of pain caused. The experiences point, I believe, to something profound about our understanding of the Church as religious brothers. While our professed theology of Church is probably quite consistent with the democratic emphases of Vatican II's pastoral and dogmatic constitutions, our lived ecclesiology may be somewhat alienated from the Church itself. No doubt, many brothers would insist that their alienation, if any, is alienation from the strictly institutional structures of the Church. Such a critique of the Church institutions has become a commonplace feature of post-Vatican II Catholic life. Nevertheless, the ways in which brothers (Christian Brothers and all others) have escaped notice and even remained on the sidelines in Church-political struggles may suggest an experience of alienation which is more profound than a simple critique of institutions.

It's All Your Fault! or:
Allowing Ourselves to Forget

BEING FORGOTTEN AND FORGETTING are not confined solely to members of religious orders or aspirants to public ministry — as the preceding incidents might suggest. The dynamic of forgetfulness, in fact, touches the experience of all Church members and this forms a bond linking the experiences of religious and laity. This bond stretches across the gap artificially created by the dichotomies of language — religious and lay being an example of such a dichotomy. The dynamic is evident even in the ways that so-called ordinary Church members experience the routine events of parish life, especially at the celebration of the Eucharist. An example may illustrate.

For several consecutive weeks during the past summer I had the opportunity to vacation with my family at a seaside resort where my family has spent part of the summer for the past thirty-five years. My parents had been very active in the fund-raising that built the parish's first large worship space — a hall which doubled for bingo (no surprise there!). Within the past five years, the parish undertook yet another fund-raising campaign and financed the design and construction of a modern, attractive church large enough to accomodate the huge numbers of summer visitors who regularly pack the church and who keep its Sunday collections quiet (as one old parish priest had once enjoined the congregation!). Two summers ago, the jovial pastor who had spearheaded the building of the new church was transferred and replaced with a more reserved, even dour, type.

The Sunday readings for the weeks in which I joined my family at the shore were very hard readings — hard on the people to whom Jesus is speaking in the Gospels, hard on the congregation who hears the text today, and hard, no doubt, on the person who preaches. The Gospels to which I am referring are those for the Nineteenth through the Twenty-Second Sundays of Ordinary Time in the C-Cycle: Luke 12:32-48 (a parable of watchful and careless servants); Luke 12:49-53 (the household divided against itself by the gospel); Luke 13:22-30 (the difficulty of entering heaven through its very narrow door); Luke 14:7-14 (the dinner where the proud guest is humbled). It would be appropriate for the homilist to challenge the congregation to live up to the demands of discipleship in the light of these readings. To do otherwise would be avoiding the task of proclamation.

The pastor preached at three of the Sunday Masses that I attended during that four-week span of time. And each week his theme was the same: the congregation was not fulfilling its financial responsibilities to their parish away from home and was, moreover, disrespectful to God and to the church by its manner of dress, lateness, early departures from liturgy, carelessness with the appointments of the church and on and on through a seemingly endless list of don'ts. Just to be sure he was heard, he repeated many of his criticisms in the church bulletin. In a particularly noteworthy entry, he went so far as to seem to blame, at least in part, the congregation for the fact that his assistant would be assigned to other duties for the off-season months:

> . . . Father . . . will not be able to say either daily Mass, so down the road we anticipate having to cut back to one daily Mass unless we are assigned an additional priest! We asked you to pray for vocations, but maybe we have to ask more often that you pray a little harder.

Typical of the kind of attitude which seemed to inspire the pastor's homilies was his closing comment on the first of those August Sundays. After having scolded the congregation for fifteen minutes during what should have been the homily, he interrupted the Rite of Dismissal for a comment before the final blessing. He began by saying that many people probably expected him to apologize for his display of anger during the homily, but that he had no intention of doing so. Then he reminded the assembly, for one last time, of their laxness; only then did he mercifully give the blessing and end the liturgy.

Many of the pastor's complaints were justified. People do attend liturgy in less than their best clothing — shorts, bathing suits and even bare feet are common. Late arrivals and early departures distract everyone and can break the concentration and flow of any liturgy, whether at a resort or in a city parish. But the fault, and the clericalism it revealed, was in the insistent repetition of the list of sins committed by the people who come not to hear that they are careless and indifferent believers, but who come to break the bread of the Word of God broken and made available for them and to share the bread and cup of salvation. This kind of judgmental finger-pointing is all too familiar to Catholics; and sadly, it too often passes for preaching.

What highlighted this experience even more starkly was a homily delivered about one month later by the campus minister who was the chaplain at the university where I teach. This priest, himself a member of a religious community composed of both brothers and priests, began his homily by recalling his own re-actions to homilies he had heard during the same four-week period in August. Like me, he had felt put off by the tone in the preaching — placing blame, putting the congregation in its place, of "telling it like it is" but without the preacher's including himself in the situation. On that September Sunday, the campus preacher modeled a completely non-clerical approach by identifying himself with the very matters put before the congregation in the readings. Simply by including himself in the challenge and grace of the Scriptures, he overcame the alienation that can intrude in the relationship between preacher and community and thereby became a countersign to a clerical style of preaching.

Perhaps clericalism is not the right name for the kind of experience with which these vignettes from a series of recent summer Sundays confront me. Maybe other names would be more appropriate. Perhaps the pastor's own life had been wounded by years of being forced to be separated, to "read the riot act" to the congregation, in general to conform to the congregation's expectations of his behavior. Clericalism however seems an appropriate name because of the relationship between the speaker and listeners and the very passive way that the listeners, week after week, accepted the criticism and condemnations delivered by one who was presumed to know better about what they should do before God in their religious lives. What is being forgotten here is the adult experience of everyone involved — preacher *and* congregation — as well as the responsibility that adults have for their lives and their faith.

Remembering/Overcoming the Forgetfulness

THESE VIGNETTES and my interpretations of them are not the end of the story. In fact, they really constitute the beginning of the story. It is our religious heritage *to remember* in order to empower ourselves for the future. In this way, our remembering connotes the experience of the two forlorn disciples on the road to Emmaus. Alone, the two could not penetrate the significance of the events surrounding Jesus' death. From their perspectives, Jesus was dead and their hope dashed. When joined by the stranger, the two review the same events for his benefit but he unlocks the meanings and transforms them into witnesses to his risen presence.

We remember these experiences of clericalism not to lick the wounds, but to prepare to act creatively in the future. We remember so that we do not become trapped in the cycle of forgetfulness and forgetting that characterizes so much of our Christian living. The creative action that our time in history requires must express our shared mission and ministry as baptized followers of Christ, a mission and ministry which demands solidarity with all who suffer oppression.

Perhaps I exaggerate to list clericalism as a form of oppression. But I do not think so. The dynamic of forgetting and forgetfulness creates a subtle form of oppression, one so subtle that it is most often not identified as such. Recall, though, the many brothers who encounter the blatant demands of a system which requires and rewards only self-effacing service at the pleasure of priests. Remember the time brothers have been forgotten by being omitted from the list of contributors to the life of the Church. Recall too the times that brothers have forgotten their fellow sisters and brothers by not witnessing to their solidarity by striving for equality of status in religious communities and throughout the Church. And finally remember experiences of finger-pointing, when those ''who know best'' tell us how to be religious, holy and faithful. Surely these experiences are forms of oppression for they are times when faithful believers are prevented by a form of clericalism from living out the mission to which they have been committed at baptism.

Observations from the Monastic Tradition

JEROME THEISEN, O.S.B.

T HIS CHAPTER represents my own experience of clericalism in monastic life. I will confine my observations to the way in which clerics and non-clerics have related in Saint John's Abbey, since my knowledge of other religious communities is not extensive. I assume, however, that my perceptions find parallels in other places where brothers and priests constitute one religious institute.

My experience of clericalism reaches back more than thirty-five years, to the days after high school when I was reflecting on the possibility of priesthood and/or religious life for myself. I never considered the religious brotherhood very seriously, partly because I was not personally acquainted with any religious brother, but more directly because the religious brother did not strike me as a person of status and importance. I felt called to the priesthood, it is true, but I noted the rank and honors which accrued to the clerics; the functions of the priest appeared more significant and noteworthy than those of the religious brothers.

My fleeting impressions were correct. When I entered the clerical novitiate of Saint John's Abbey in 1951, I found that the youngest clerical novices entered a different formation program from that designed for the lay brothers; our priesthood orientation set us apart in living quarters, classes, rank, and privileges.

More was expected of the clerical novice in matters of intelligence, education, and health. He was obliged to have finished at least two years of college; he was expected to have enough mental acumen to complete a course in philosophy and theology; he needed the physical stamina and integrity to function as a priest.

The brother novice, on the other hand, was not obliged to have completed any particular level of education, though he might have finished high school or some trade school. He was accepted for his desire to live the monastic life and his ability to work at some task that contributed to the well-being of the monastery or in one of its apostolates.

It was generally assumed without too much reflection that the brother novice was less able in matters of book learning, speech, and administration. The lesser talent was acceptable because he was not destined for the priesthood or for positions of authority in the monastery. If he did have scholastic aptitude, he was often encouraged to study for the priesthood; then, of course, he ceased to be a brother.

Once I, as a clerical novice, professed monastic vows, I moved to a place in the monastery called the clericate and I myself was called a cleric. Ironically, I was called *frater*, the Latin word for brother; in fact, even as a novice I was given the title of frater novice. Since the abbreviation of the word *frater* is fr., I had a title that appeared very much like that of the ordained priest: Father (abbreviated Fr.). I was required to wear a Roman collar from the very day of monastic profession; indeed, I was eager to wear it.

The collar, the name, the studies, the living quarters, and the rank, set me, the cleric, off from the brother. Ours were priesthood studies with some manual work in the afternoon, on Sundays, and during the summer months. Theirs was manual labor from the first days of their entry into the monastery as candidates and novices; sometimes it was the menial task of cleaning rooms or making the beds of the priests. Ours was the Latin choir, the full celebration of the divine office as arranged in the *Rule of Benedict* (though not at the times of the day and night prescribed by Benedict). Theirs was a shorter version of the office in English, presided over, it is true, by the brothers themselves. Ours was the daily sung or recited community Mass. Theirs was a separate communion mass and the serving of private Masses for the priests, though novices and clerics, too, served for private celebrations of the Eucharist. Only on Sundays did the whole monastic community come together for Mass and vespers, but even then the brothers were at a disadvantage when it came to singing the Gregorian melodies and Latin psalms.

The largely separate life of brother and cleric left me with the impression that my vocation was more important to the Church and to the monastery. I assumed that the brother could at times get the impression that his life and his work were less important to the local church and to the monastic community.

During my early years in the monastery I noticed that the brother did not participate directly in our two main apostolates: education and parochial ministry. I say directly because they labored hard and daily in supportive roles to maintain the buildings and to staff the offices. At the same time they provided much physical labor in our missions and in newly founded and dependent priories.

The brother lacked the proper education to teach in our schools and to minister in our parishes; very few, in fact, had attended college before coming to the monastery. Moreover, it was assumed that the brothers were not proper candidates for graduate school where they could have earned the requisite degrees for teaching. Parochial ministry was even farther from their sights.

Simply stated, the clerics and priests attended schools so that they could obtain the proper credentials for priestly ministry and teaching while the brothers were not directed to schools or college or advanced degrees. This situation resulted in an educational imbalance that generally followed the lines of cleric and non-cleric, or priest and brother: the cleric was highly educated while the brother was not.

It must be stated, however, that this clear-cut division between the educated cleric and the non-educated brother was beginning to blur in the 1950's as one or more brothers came to the monastery with college degrees and began to teach in our schools.

The education and employment imbalance between the cleric and the non-cleric carried other ramifications. The cleric traveled more for purposes of education and ministry. It was not unusual for the cleric to pursue higher degrees in cities like Rome, Paris, Munich, or Washington, D.C. Such travel was not open to the non-cleric. Furthermore, parochial ministry generally obliged the cleric to have a car, to travel, and to be absent from the monastery for months and years.

Thus, to be a cleric gave one greater access to foreign travel and assignments away from the monastery. To be a brother provided one with the greater probability of living and working in the abbey.

The living quarters of the brother were poorer in quality than those of the priests. The clerical novice and the monk seminarian, it must be noted, also had simple living quarters: large dormitories and study halls. But it was assumed that the professed brother generally did not need much more than a bed, a desk, a locker, and a chair. He could withdraw books from the common library and read the magazines in the common recreation room (which was also separate from that of the fathers, clerics, and the clerical novices). The brother lived simply, having very few clothes and very few creature comforts (as they were called); for example, the brothers could not smoke cigarettes as could the clerics once they were ordained to the priesthood. It seemed to be expected that the brother would live more simply than the priest and the cleric, that he would observe more fully the vow of poverty which entailed simplicity of life and the community of goods.

Before Vatican Council II another imbalance existed in the monastery, an imbalance in access to positions of authority and power. The brother did not share in the deliberations of the community's chapter, the business assembly of the priests and clerics; he had no forum of expression nor vote on matters that pertained to the well-being of the monastery.

The brother could not hold an official position in the monastery such as abbot, prior, or subprior, though he could be a dean of brothers with some very limited authority. Nor could he be elected to the council of seniors, the immediate advisory body of the abbot and the board of directors of the corporation. He could, of course, talk directly and privately to the officials of the monastery, to the council of seniors and to members of the chapter.

The absence of a chapter vote brought about the unspoken assumption that the brothers, always in junior position, did not have to be consulted about plans for the development of the monastery. They were available to implement the plans discussed and voted on by the clerics and priests. Of course, a certain level of consultation continued, especially on an informal basis, but as a matter of policy the brothers were not in a position to direct the growth and vision of the monastery.

Clericalism also directed ways of thought and speech. It was assumed that the brother was an easier target for correction. Since he was always junior in rank, the brother was not infrequently subject to the commands of the cleric. It is only honest to admit that some of the correction was abusive, especially since the brother had little choice but to accept the correction of a cleric.

The junior position also implied that the brother received the ministrations of the priest, for the priest by reason of his office dispensed advice and sacraments. The brother sought counsel, instruction, and the sacraments from him.

Before Vatican II the monks, both clerical and non-clerical, professed monastic vows in an atmosphere of simple and quiet celebration, and no one commemorated the anniversaries of profession. The ordination of monks, however, entailed a different situation: the ordination rite and the first Mass involved much solemnity, especially in the church which the priest monk regarded as his home parish. Moreover, the priests celebrated jubilees, in particular the twenty-fifth and the fiftieth anniversaries of ordination.

It occurs to me now that the brother remained in a junior position all his life, that he was always lower in rank, never given responsible and official positions of authority. In a sense he always remained a second-class citizen of the monastery, but not even a citizen with voting rights. He was attached to the monastery, lived the monastic life, but did not carry the canonical name of monk. He was known as a lay brother (*frater laicus* or *frater conversus*).

What did such a status do to the brother's sense of self-worth and self-appreciation? His personal development could hardly have been unaffected by the status, but in spite of their lower rank many if not most of the brothers developed into mature, dedicated religious. Did the stable family backgrounds, from which most of them came, support them in situations that were less than enhancing of their personal development? Did their steady monastic life provide them with rich religious growth? Did their cohesiveness as a group (common prayer, shared recreation, like status) assist them in their sense of self-worth?

Up to this point I have enumerated various official and negative factors of the life of the brother as compared to the cleric of the monastery. It needs to be said that the relationship between the brother and the cleric or priest was often mutually respectful, affectionate, and appreciative. The brother craftsman was well regarded for his talents and for his contributions to the well-being of the community and its apostolates. The artist brother could pursue his work with a great deal of admiration.

In his heart of hearts the cleric generally recognized that many of the brothers were steeped in wisdom and piety, that they were dedicated to a life of faith and monastic behavior. In fact, many brothers were envied for their solid devotion and their daily routine of monastic life. In many ways they adhered more closely to the prescriptions of the *Rule of Benedict* than did many of the clerics and priests. They often lived balanced lives of seclusion, simplicity, prayer and reading.

The brothers were not without regular instruction in the monastic and religious life. A master was assigned to them for purposes of instruction and to act as their immediate superior. Of course, the master was not one of their own but a priest who could give them theological and spiritual conferences. Thus, the brothers were not neglected in religious instruction, but they did not have access to the theology courses of the seminary program.

The theological and spiritual ferment surrounding Vatican Council II (1962-1965) brought about momentous changes in the monastery and in the way brothers related to the clerics or the priests. This is not to say that there was a sharp break before and after the council. Some changes, for example, in common liturgy or in work assignments, were in evidence to some degree before the council, and others did not take effect until some years after the council. But in general it is true to say that the council itself formed the great watershed of change.

The most far-reaching change centered on the "monastic" characterization of the brother. He was no longer regarded as a lay-brother but a canonically recognized monk of the abbey. Any person who entered the monastery and professed monastic vows was really and canonically a monk, no matter whether he intended to study for the priesthood or not. This change, of course, was a return to the original inspiration of the monastic movement and of the *Rule of Benedict*. Benedict allowed priests to make monastic profession and to live in the monastery; he also designated some monks for ordination to the priesthood; but it was assumed that all monks formed one brotherhood and that priests were obliged to live the monastic life as any other monk in the monastery.

Vatican Council II unified our monastic community and brought it back to Benedict's original arrangement. One formation program served the needs of all candidates whether they intended to study for the priesthood or not. Rank in the monastery was no longer determined by ordination but by time of entry into the monastery or by the date of profession. As a result the whole community took on a different appearance as brother stood next to father in choir or ate next to the cleric at table.

Changes in canonical status and rank brought about or accompanied other significant alterations in the life of the monastery. The most important was liturgical. Whereas pre-Vatican II days witnessed two choirs in the monastery, one in English for the brothers, the other in Latin for the clerics, the liturgical movement that reached its high point in the council advocated a vernacular celebration of the liturgy of the hours. With the shift from Latin to English in the liturgy, the brother, who was generally unschooled in Latin, could more easily join the clerics in one choir of monks for the celebration of the work of God (*opus Dei*). I say more easily because the brother, accustomed to a shorter and different pattern of prayer, was now confronted with the full gamut of psalms, canticles, and Scripture readings.

It was heartening to observe that the whole monastic community could come together for the Eucharist and the liturgy of the hours. The shift in language brought the community together for its most characteristic and regular duty: the celebration of the divine office.

While the integration of the choirs for the divine office proceeded relatively smoothly, the same cannot be said for the celebration of the Eucharist. The vast majority of the monks, it is true, received with joy the introduction of English into the celebration of

Mass. The vernacular, in fact, made it easier for the entire community to celebrate a common Eucharist. The Latin language, which often served as the characteristic mark of the cleric, gave way to the English language, though it continued to be used in some hymns and motets.

But more was at issue then the Latin language. It was the celebrant of the Mass himself. Priests were celebrants at Mass; brothers were not. The Eucharist, therefore, became a time when the division of the community into brothers and priests was most apparent.

The problem did not appear so much in the celebration of private Masses. Before Vatican Council II a priest of the monastery, unless he was scheduled for the conventual Mass or parochial duties, usually offered a private Mass with the attendance of another monk, often a brother. It had long been part of the daily life of the brother to serve the private Masses of the fathers. This practice did not cease with the coming of Vatican II and the introduction of concelebration in the daily conventual Mass of the monastery. Some priests disliked concelebration and continued to offer private Masses, often served by brothers. This situation continues to the present day; a few priests still offer Mass privately and a few brothers still serve them.

The area that most exaggerated the relationship between the brothers and the priests was concelebration, a new type of which was introduced by the reforms of Vatican Council II. It was assumed in some circles before the council that concelebration would solve the problem of having dozens of priests attend a conventual Mass and then celebrate private Masses more or less at the same time in a variety of chapels. When I entered the monastery, it was the practice of the priests to "meditate" but not receive communion during the conventual Mass and then to receive communion at their own privately celebrated Mass. It was assumed, I repeat, that concelebration would eleminate this incongruous situation.

But the reality was otherwise. Before Vatican Council II the brothers attended the Sunday conventual Mass but not those of the other days of the week. For the first time in memory they were scheduled to attend the daily conventual Mass which was normally concelebrated by a large crowd of priests. The conventual Mass, therefore, became the time of the day when the difference between brother and cleric was brought to fullest expression.

Concelebration placed many priests around the altar vested in chasubles, pronouncing out loud words of the eucharistic prayer with the presider, and engaged in various gestures. If the number of priests was large and if they surrounded the altar, they effectively blocked the view of the altar. The brothers and others who attended the Mass from a greater distance had to look past and around a group of concelebrating priests. The brothers got the impression that the conventual Mass was a clerical Mass, that is, celebrated by and for the convenience of the priests.

These complaints on the part of the brothers brought about various adjustments in the manner in which concelebration took place. After a time the concelebrants no longer vested in chasuble but dressed more simply in alb and stole. They did not come forward to surround the altar for the eucharistic prayer but remained in their places (taking seats in the choir stalls for the whole Mass except to come forward for communion). They no longer pronounced the words of the anaphora in a loud voice but concelebrated in a nearly inaudible tone of voice. Also, it became customary not to have concelebration for the most important eucharistic liturgy of the week, the community Mass of Sunday.

The adjustments were viewed as attempts to de-clericalize the Mass, and they were coupled with endeavors to involve the brothers more directly in the ceremonies of the Mass. Thereafter brothers were regularly scheduled to read the Scriptures (the first lesson, not the gospel), to lead the singing, and to assist in the distribution of communion. Especially on Sundays the brothers entered more fully into the celebration of the conventual Mass by ministering to the presider, by assisting in the distribution of communion, by announcing the Mass on the local radio station, by ushering students and visitors, and by entering the church in procession with the whole monastic community. In point of fact, both brothers and clerics took up the various tasks related to the celebration of the Eucharist.

The Sunday conventual Mass, which is open to students and visitors, has been perfected to the point where it is fairly successful at a time when the whole community (except those who are occupied in parochial or some other duties) is able to celebrate the Lord's supper around one table, and this under the leadership of one celebrant. Priests take turns celebrating the Sunday liturgy. It must be acknowledged, however, that some priests still prefer to celebrate Mass privately, even on Sundays, and they thus draw a few brothers to their service. A few other brothers prefer to avoid the conventual Mass and to continue what they know best: the private or small group Mass.

Clericalism in the Mass, here understood as a celebration of the Mass that accents the place of the priest, was only one factor, even if a large factor, in the problems of the daily conventual Mass. Other factors included the time of day for the community Mass (a shift from early morning to late morning or late afternoon), the quality and frequency of the homily (they were non-existent before Vatican Council II, not even on Sundays), the type of song at the liturgy, the kind of bread used in the celebration, the placement and presence of students and visitors, and the sign of peace.

A larger issue, which can only be mentioned here, is the place of the Eucharist in the spirituality of the monks, both priests and brothers. The *Rule of Benedict* carefully arranges for celebration of the liturgy of the hours but says very little about Mass and communion. Presumably the monks of Benedict's monastery celebrated Mass on Sundays and received communion in some short service on weekdays. In other words, early Benedictine spirituality in matters of time and schedule centered more on the

divine office and *lectio divina* (prayerful reading) than on the
Mass. After a few centuries the daily community Mass (sometimes
more than one) took on added significance in the horarium of the
monastery. That is not to say that the development was illegiti-
mate, but it is to point out the inspiration of early Benedictine
monasticism and the problems that developed since that day.

The non-ordained monk (a clearer designation of the brother
since we are all brothers in the monastery) became more involved
in the celebration of the divine office. Before Vatican Council II
only priests functioned as prayer leaders in choir and at table. After
the council all monks were offered the possibility of leading
prayers for the liturgy of the hours and at table. They were also
given the opportunity to read the Scriptures and other writings at
the divine office.

While clericalism in the celebration of the Eucharist remained
a problem after Vatican Council II, I am happy to report that it
lessened considerably in work assignments. New candidates coming to the monastery were given the possibility of working in a
variety of areas, some of which were formerly closed to them, e.g.,
university teaching and administration. Both brother and priest
now engage in a wide range of work assignments: high school
teaching and administration, garden work, writing and editing, etc.
Only recently a non-ordained monk was appointed to an official
position in the monastery and another to the office of prior of a
dependent monastery. But the office of abbot is still closed to the
non-ordained monk.

It is encouraging to note another phenomenon in recent years:
able-bodied brothers and priests take their turns in performing
household tasks of the monastery such as waiting on table, preparing breakfast trays for the sick and elderly, ministering at the
Eucharist, cleaning sections of the monastery, serving at the local
fire department. Priests and brothers see the need to serve each
other in community.

For about ten to fifteen years after the council a certain spirit of anti-clericalism and a struggle against priestly privilege were detectable in the monastery; this was accompanied by residual disparagements of the non-ordained monk on the part of some priests. Other clerics and priests, however, took up the "cause" of the brothers, sympathized with their struggles, and lived a life similar to theirs. The anti-clerical spirit never caused a serious split in the community, but at times it resulted in cutting words and caused antagonism between the two groups.

The anti-clerical feeling among some of the younger monks made it difficult for those who wished to study for the priesthood. To study for the priesthood seemed like a capitulation to the clerical status. This attitude was not widespread but it was present. In point of fact, after Vatican II monks continued to study for the priesthood, though fewer in number than before the council. Also, the proportion of priesthood candidates to non-priesthood candidates changed significantly in the period after the council; while previously four out of five candidates entering the monastery were destined for the priesthood, later the proportion became about fifty percent. Perhaps fewer candidates were called to the priesthood, but it was also apparent that one did not have to undertake priestly studies to enter the full life of the monastry.

The post-Vatican II monastery witnessed much more equality in the use of cars and money and in access to graduate education and to trips. These items do not divide the brothers and the clerics; rather some fathers and brothers live rather simply and other fathers and brothers live more extravagantly.

The post-Vatican II formation program requires more theology on the part of all candidates. The junior in formation either enrolls in a full program of theology in preparation for ordination to the priesthood or he takes college or graduate theology courses to give him some framework for understanding the religious and monastic life.

The non-ordained monks, especially because of their stability, provided a cohesiveness to the monastic community in the years both before and after the council. They were the monks who worked hard to build up the physical complex of the monastery, and they were the ones who kept it going from day to day. In great measure, their steadiness and hard work carried the monastery through thé rough years after Vatican II.

Today we have a fairly unified community of monks, both ordained and non-ordained. It is true that fewer brothers than fathers are in positions of authority, but much more progress has been made in this regard, especially in education which provides the credentials for offices of leadership. In any event the more prestigious jobs are open to brothers.

The full burdens and privileges of the monastic life are open to the non-ordained monk as well as to the ordained. This means that the brothers as well as the priests can choose inobservance! Non-adherence to the norms of monastic living is no longer a clerical privilege! The brother as well as the father — and there are some of each — can live a more extravagant lifestyle, can avoid common prayer and table, can demand more travel and vacations, etc. There is now equality in the possibility of observance and inobservance!

The celebration of anniversaries was limited to priest monks before Vatican Council II. After the council the monastery stressed the primacy of the profession of monastic vows. What brings us together now in one community is not the priesthood but the desire to live the cenobitic life. As a result the profession of monastic vows is celebrated with great solemnity, indeed with too much pomp in the minds of a few monks. The community stresses initial and solemn vows, which are now open to all the monks, but also the commemoration of the anniversaries of the vows, at first only the golden jubilee but later the silver as well. The celebration of the anniversaries of vows is now a community affair while the celebration of anniversaries of ordination is hardly noticed by the community and tends to be celebrated away from the abbey, in one's home parish or in the parish of the priest's present assignment.

The recent expression of equality among the monks in the monastery stems not only from our American culture which advocates freedom, democratization, and individualism, but also from the principles of the apostle Paul who sees belief in Jesus as the great equalizer; our differences pale in comparison with our unity in Christ (cf. Gal 3:28). Our generation of candidates to monastic life does not tolerate inequities based on class or education. This attitude, in fact, returns to the norms of Saint Benedict who opposed favoritism based on education, family background, or clerical status.

Endnote

Some members of Saint John's community, especially Brother Francis Peters, Brother Dietrich Reinhart, and Father Colman Barry, commented on an early version of this chapter. I acknowledge the helpfulness of their suggestions as well as those of others in the community.

Epilogue:
A Hopeful Beginning

JORDAN HITE, T.O.R.

T HE PAPERS in this study, plus the survey of the attitudes of brothers and priests who are members of institutes of consecrated life in the United States, are the first comprehensive studies of the relationship between brothers and priests and the factors that affect the relationship. The purpose of the studies is to help us to begin to understand the vocation of each and how they relate to one another. The disciplines of history, theology, culture, psychology and canon law form a background that helps us to understand the experience from the point of view of those who have been called to the brotherhood and the perception of those who know them. I want briefly to review the ideas that made a strong impression on me and then offer some comments on the question.

As Fitz notes, history frees us from the illusion that the present practice is the one and only traditional practice. It is clear that religious life began with the Christian laity. The ordained soon joined them but only became a majority in some groups at a much later date. For Benedict and Francis the ideal relationship between brothers and priests was fraternity which resulted in equal treatment within the community. Ordination for those called to priesthood was meant to serve the brotherhood or the people of God. Even the first division of roles within the monastery was not along the lines of lay and ordained. Instead it took the form of those who were choir monks (lay and ordained) and those who assisted the choir monks to save them from the distraction of temporal business.

Although many monks became ordained to administer the sacraments as part of their mission activity, the idea of restricting governance in religious communities to the ordained was much more related to the Gregorian Reform which tried to rid the Church of secular influence over its appointments and ministry. Stripping lay rulers of jurisdiction in Church matters ultimately had the effect of eliminating lay governance in male religious communities, which over the centuries resulted in clerical leadership both in fact and then by law. The clericalization of leadership in men's communities was a fact of life by the time the Church came to the United States.

The survey of history describes a series of events that took place not only in different times but in a variety of locations and cultures. When culture is understood as how people in a given situation understand themselves, their relationships, and their ideals, with a focus on the values and meanings that people assign to their environment, we have another tool that helps us to examine the brother-priest relationship. First, to recognize that the Church itself is a culture, an environment in which we live, sheds a certain light on the relationship. Within the Church we can recognize two forms of social organization, hierarchical and egalitarian. The hierarchical has a certain order, and everyone has a role. Not everyone is capable of performing every function. The crucial principles for forming the social order are power and status. In the Church, hierarchical ordering is based on access to sacred power which to a certain extent is conferred through ordination. This divides the Church into a society of clergy and laity.

Alongside the hierarchical culture in the Church, there is also an egalitarian culture. It is a culture in which access to sacred power is not defined from within the Church according to those who are ordained and those who are not; but rather access to sacred power is based on whether one is a member of the Church or not. Thus, baptism is the boundary and not ordination. Religious institutes to a large extent are a model of the egalitarian culture in the Church. The entrance of clergy into religious institutes in early Church history had already produced moments of tension. We are now in another moment of tension. This is the product of the call of Vatican II for institutes to return to their original charism (internal) and a call to all in the Church to live out more fully their baptismal commitment (external). Both of these represent Church approval of renewal along egalitarian lines within a hierarchical Church.

The stimuli to tension do not end with the Church, as U.S. religious live in a national culture. It is a culture which is identified by egalitarianism and individualism. The egalitarianism of U.S. culture coincides with and reinforces that aspect of religious life. The individualism plus egalitarianism produces both pluralism and acceptable divisions in society that tend to undermine tradition as a stabilizing force. The acceptance among American religious of American cultural ideals means to a certain extent that their witness against the negative aspects of American life is diminished. Thus, American culture can be either a positive or negative force in striving to live the Gospel. American religious, therefore, are double heirs to an egalitarian tradition that motivates them to express basic equality in relationships.

The study of the identity of the lay brother is stimulating in its approach. The view that the call to be a brother is both dangerous and a privilege places it in a unique context. In addition the use of the historical approach: the way things were, the way things are, and the way things may be — which runs through the entire analysis — focuses on the question of identity. The designation of ''non-cleric'' is one that deprives a brother of identity. The brother's status in the hierarchical structure is a place lower than priests. The comment that brothers "hadn't gone all the way" to ordination has caused resentment among brothers. In communities where brothers and priests lived together, priests had the opportunity and stimulation of outside ministry while brothers were often limited to assisting priests or working within the community. This sometimes led to an isolated lifestyle and narrow interests. The title "lay brother" was often translated into the distinction of being unskilled or uneducated. The brother was identified as being somewhere between priest and layman. The in-between place was often unsettling and led to a lack of identity.

Today, we are experiencing the challenge of Vatican II. The effects of what has been can still be felt. Today, brothers face important choices on how to be free from the elements of the past that were obstacles to their call and yet meet the challenge of taking their place as men with an identifiable call and mission.

In the days ahead, brothers have the opportuniy to mold and form their own identity as well as to face the challenge of the world in which they live and minister. As both the theological reflection and the experiential studies show, these issues belong not only to the brothers but to the remainder of the Church as well. All of us are called to properly understand the call to be a brother so that we are part of a solution to the problem rather than an obstacle.

As I read the theological reflection and the experiential articles, they came to form one piece in my own mind. I was probably led to this conclusion by the methodology of drawing on the revelatory experience of the theologizing commmunity. In the theological study it is the express purpose of the study to do so while in the experiential articles it is implicit in the individual contributor's experience as Church.

The articles are nicely balanced since two are brothers (one in a brothers' community, one in a mixed community) two are priests in a mixed community (including the theological article), and two are from those who have experienced brothers from outside a men's community. They are all remarkable in the way they substantiate and witness to the issues noted in the other articles. Here we have first-hand evidence of the problems of identity, structure, and equality. The theological reflection phrases the problem accurately by challenging the Church to "bring the transforming power of the gospel to bear on this stressful and not fully redeemed ecclesial situation."

It is interesting to hear the observation of a priest in a functional sense viewing himself as a part-time priest (when engaged in the ministries only a priest can perform) and a full-time Christian and religious. Admittedly, this is not the way most think, either priests or third parties. However, it does place emphasis on a perception that seems to be the idea of most members of religious institutes: that a man is called first to be a member of a community and second to specify his vocation as brother or priest.

This perception is a good introduction to the canonical study. It deals squarely with the idea of total equality within a religious institute. The conclusions of the articles are clear. Under present Church law brothers are prevented from becoming superiors over clerics. A brother may hold the office of superior only if he receives a dispensation from the Holy See. In religious institutes which began with equal rights and privileges for members this law represents a violation of their charism, to which they were asked to return by Vatican II. Institutes which in fact restricted the rights of brothers, even if for good cause, now believe that this situation has changed so that equality is the proper expression of their life. They find that the law is an obstacle, that it is inadequate and denies reality by recognizing only two types of institutes, lay and clerical, when in fact many are mixed and have been so since the time of their origin. Institutes can deal with the "jurisdictional" matters reserved to priests if they elect a brother superior along the lines of the dispensations given by CRIS and the constitutions they have approved for some groups. It is time for this solution to be offered to institutes by way of their own law rather than by dispensation.

Along with the other authors of this volume, I am hopeful that in the days ahead the insights, observations and questions presented here will aid the Church in discovering again the importance of the call to be a brother. The fact that this important vocation has gotten lost and been a source of pain for many brothers is incentive enough in itself. We need to return to the ideal of Benedict and Francis that the ideal relationship between brothers and priests is that of fraternity. When fraternity is the starting point the specific ministries and functions of brothers and priests within the fraternity are founded on the most basic of relationships. This relationship is consistent with the first and primary sacramental relationship within the Church, that of baptism. A true understanding of the sacraments means that they complement each other and provide the foundation for other relationships within the Church.

Even though ordination allows the priest the privilege and responsibility of certain ministries and Church law reserves certain legal matters to priests, this does not mean priests have a "higher place" in the Church. The performance of these functions is meant to be done according to the biblical norms of "humble service." Jesus came among us as one who was meek and humble of heart. This, of course, is the goal of all Christians including priests and also should be the perception of those who relate to priests, even though certain canonical, social, historical and cultural factors have led to the view that priests are "higher." The call to be a priest is not devalued by the norm of "humble service" but rather finds its true place according to the mind of Jesus.

The responses to the survey questions offer us more detailed material for prayer and reflection than we have ever had access to before. For example, 77% of those responding thought that priests were more highly valued than brothers in both Church and lay activities, and 72% agreed that the lay public were less aware of the charisms of the brotherhood than the priesthood. On the other hand 60% believed that aside from sacramental differences, brothers do not have a lesser status than priests and 83% thought that ordination merely reflects a different vocation than the brotherhood. A series of questions on the subject of holding office was very revealing. Eighty-seven percent believed brothers would have a more positive image in the Church if they could hold any office in the community. Among members of mixed institutes (brothers and priests) 86% were in favor of brothers being able to be local superiors and 70% were in favor of a brother being eligible to be a major superior or a supreme moderator. In the section of the survey answered only by brothers 78% thought that all offices in an institute should be open to both brothers and priests.

Hopefully this study will find its way not only to religious communities, especially to house meetings and chapters, but also to the laity. The issues presented by this study are broader than "in-house" relationships and Church law. If the experiential papers indicate anything, they show how the perception of the brotherhood by the Church at large has an impact on the brother's call.

Both the Congregation for Religious and Secular Institutes and the Church itself are well aware of the issues presented here. The Union of Superiors General has already begun to study the question. The papers here are meant to complement all the other studies and discussions. This activity shows the sensitivity and interest of the Church at its highest level. The fact that this study will be part of the Church's ongoing work and be a contribution to the information it can gather from its universal experience is a hopeful note on which to conclude. All this effort represents an excellent beginning which should bring positive results in the near future.

III. Analysis of Responses

Issues of Status, Power and Role Differentiation in Male Religious Identity: Results of a National Survey

DAVID NYGREN, C.M.
RALPH L. PIEDMONT

Introduction

W HEN VINCENT DE PAUL exhorted the brothers and priests of his community "to live in the manner of very dear brothers," he clearly intended that the Vincentian identity be rooted in the mission which priests and brothers shared in common. He distinguished the functions of brothers and priests while insisting upon equality between them. And such respect was expected even though separation between brothers and priests was also common to their way of life.

These papers have repeatedly acknowledged that fraternity among brothers and priests may lack the force of structure and law to fulfill the ideals espoused by founders of congregations. Similarly, among communities whose members are all brothers, there appears to be less internal tension between brothers but significant difficulties between these brothers and the priests with whom they work. Various writers have proposed that the relationships between them may be explained by analyzing the degrees of power which accompany their roles, the perceived status which accompanies their functions, their educational backgrounds, and even their personality types. The accusation of "clericalism" still pervades some interactions between priests and others when priests are perceived to unfairly influence, control, or exact privileges because of their self-inspired dominance. Whatever the source of the perceived tension, the dynamics between priests and brothers expressed in these papers provide a window into the changing shape of the North American Church.

This chapter describes the results of a national survey of brothers and priests designed to explore the dynamics of their relationships. The major themes examined in the research were developed through interviews, the papers presented in this book, and from the authors' experiences of religious life. The issues identified for consideration relate to general perceptions of both brother and priest roles, the impact of ordination on perception, ecclesial perceptions of various role functions, and the distinctive qualities of role interaction.

These papers have suggested that tension between brothers and priests may be experienced by either group when roles, responsibilities or status are perceived to be distributed inequitably. Since Vatican II the complementary nature of lay and clerical spirituality and mission have attempted to minimize distinctions between groups while reinforcing the distinct role responsibilities necessary to maintain Church structures as they currently exist.

When viewed as a social system, the Church can be described by analyzing what various members do, what they believe in, and how they symbolically express what they believe. Social systems like the Church function through complex implicit and explicit structures of relationships. Certain attitudes tend to govern behaviors and interactions within these systems. Without the Church structure, characteristic roles and role expectations define the interdependent nature of people committed to a single mission. While the role expectations of priests have changed considerably, the beliefs of the larger body of the U.S. Church concerning the roles and responsibilities given to the laity have changed drastically. With time and deliberate action the symbols and structures which define their changed roles will likely emerge.

Moreover, in congregations of religious men, the role of the brother has evolved to include many of the ministerial and pastoral functions once considered the domain of the priest. In addition congregations have worked extensively in revising their constitutions to eliminate the perceived imbalance of power, opportunities, and role responsibilities between brothers and priests. Although the spirit of equality has increased, the ability to share authority, for example, by allowing brothers to hold any office in the congregation, has not met with official ecclesiastical approval. Nevertheless, fraternity or brotherhood has become for many congregations the primary descriptor of membership, and language of equality now supersedes images of power which once circumscribed the presbyteral role even in religious congregations.

In the previous chapter, Hite suggested that the crux of the tension between brothers and priests lies at the intersection of hierarchical structures supported by power and status differences and egalitarian structures which engage emergent leadership within the Church based on the fundamental equality of believers in baptism. In the years since Vatican II the Church has continued to refine the centrality of the mission amidst diverse role functions. It has challenged priests to collaborate, delegate, and share authority within the bounds of Canon Law. And priests report feeling caught between the assumptions of two competing foundations: hierarchical authority and collaborative models of governance. To the extent that they exercise their role function in relation to a hierarchical social order, others appear to feel subordinated. And when they collaborate in ministry, they are often perceived as undermining authority or as being weak leaders.

The social and ecclesial forces which have changed the role identity of brothers and priests provide a complex platform for exploratory research. The rich experiences recounted in these papers led us to ask how prevalent these attitudes may be in the Church. What attitudes, behaviors, and structures are shaping the efforts of brothers and priests to live in equality and fraternity? Clearly the dynamics between priests and brothers in religious congregations have broad implications for the Church and are influenced by other social and ecclesial factors. The purpose of this report was to examine the perceptions of the role of the brother within the Church and to provide an estimation of the degree to which issues of status, identity and role differentiation influence relationships between brothers and priests. The scope of this exploratory research was limited to male religious in order to better understand their experience of a primary relationship of community. Subsequent research on the relationship of priests to other groups in the Church, especially women, as well as the relationship of brothers to the laity, could highlight the dynamic changes currently shaping vocational commitment and religious life in the North American Church.

Method

THE PURPOSE OF THIS SECTION is to outline the procedures employed in the development of the questionnaire, the sampling procedures and the amount of confidence that can be placed in the obtained result.

THE QUESTIONNAIRE

The questionnaire consisted of approximately 120 questions grouped around 8 areas:

These areas were distilled from the many issues generated by the previous works in this volume, from interviews and from the authors' experiences of religious life. The questions explored extensively perceptions of the roles of brothers and priests. Of particular interest were perceptions of power and status differences and the tension they create between priests and brothers.

The actual items were developed by the authors after reviewing the previous chapters and conducting 9 structured interviews with a group of brothers and priests. Responses were marked in either a "Yes-No" format or on a 1 to 4, disagree-agree, scale. The original instrument was screened by a panel of both brothers and priests (this panel consisted of the editorial board established by CMSM to conduct this study) and appropriate revisions were effected. The questionnaire was then pretested on a small group of brothers and priests and their comments noted. Most were quite positive about the instrument and saw it as offering an opportunity to open a dialogue on a very salient issue. Again, certain modifications were made to some items in an attempt to improve clarity. The survey then underwent a final screening by the original panel and their approval was received. At this point the survey was mailed to our randomly selected sample.

SAMPLING PROCEDURES

Individuals eligible for participation in this study were those whose Order was a member of the Conference of Major Superiors of Men (CMSM). A total population of over 25,000 (18,144 priests, 7,000 brothers) was targeted. From a current directory of religious congregations, a simple random sample of 2,672 individuals (1,360 priests, 1,312 brothers) received the survey questionnaire.

Those surveyed were sent a questionnaire, a stamped return envelope, and a cover letter. The cover letter contained an explanation of the purpose of the questionnaire (to evaluate the relationship between priests and brothers in the Church) and an assurance of confidentiality.

The mailing to all 2,672 recipients occurred in February 1987. The final response rate of usable surveys was 52% (685 priests and 718 brothers). An additional 1% of the surveys were from individuals who were in formation and were not included in any analysis. Approximately 10% of the surveys were returned unanswered because the recipient had moved, passed away, or was not capable of responding.

QUALITY OF THE SURVEY DATA

Given that there are no current and accurate listings of the demographic characteristics of members of CMSM organizations, it is impossible to compare the features of this sample to a criterion that would determine its actual representativeness. However, the results of the study can be viewed with a reasonably high degree of confidence for several reasons. First, a response rate which exceeds 50% on a national survey provides a strong assurance that the results are not seriously biased by the lack of response from a substantial portion of the membership.

Since there is no current demographic information available, the actual characteristics of the respondents are presented in Tables 1 and 2 for brothers and priests, respectively. The degree of consistency of these results adds further confidence in these survey findings as accurately reflecting the selected population. Both groups reflect a relatively older, predominantly white population. That both brothers and priests rate the average age of the members of their community to be approximately 53, suggests that this older sample is not the product of any sampling bias but actually reflects a smaller number of young religious members. Although both groups are highly educated, the higher percentage of priests with bachelor degrees and above reflects the greater emphasis placed on educational preparation for the priesthood. Further, that there is a higher percentage of priests involved in a parish ministry and a higher percentage of brothers involved in a ministry of manual labor is consistent with the expectations assigned to the traditional roles of each group.

The great amount of attention and effort given to the questionnaire by the respondents is another factor contributing to the confidence that can be placed in these results. Many respondents added comments to emphasize specific concerns. In some instances with older or physically incapacitated individuals, other community members were assigned to read the questionnaire and note the respondent's answers. It is clear that respondents made a very serious effort to answer the questions in an open and honest manner. Most respondents commented on the importance of this study to the future of religious life in the United States. With few exceptions, the respondents critiqued the questionnaire favorably and, in some instances, provided additional material in an attempt to augment the research endeavor.

Finally, based on the size of the original population and the number of responses, statistically speaking, we can be 99% confident that the values obtained in this survey are within 5 percentage points of the actual population values. In other words, if

66% of the brothers in our sample agree with a particular statement, one can be 99% certain that between 61% and 71% of *all* brothers agree with that statement.

Major Findings

GIVEN THE LENGTH of this survey, it is impossible to provide, within the limits of this chapter, a complete presentation of all the findings. Rather, the major issues that emerged will be presented in a more detailed fashion. The data relating to brothers and priests will be presented and discussed separately. At the end of this section conclusions will be drawn for all the data combined.

FACTOR ANALYSIS

The principal method of evaluating the results was factor analysis. This method is a data reduction technique, the purpose of which is to reduce a large number of items to a smaller, more manageable amount of 'factors.' These 'factors' represent groupings of items that all share something in common. What this 'communality' is, is determined through an examination of the items in each group. A factor analysis was performed separately on the responses for brothers and priests and the resulting factors are presented in Tables 3 and 4. The names of these factors are arbitrary and reflect the authors' interpretations of the item groupings. Other titles could be equally appropriate. Nevertheless, these factors represent salient dimensions for both brothers and priests. Scores were found for each respondent by adding up their responses on the items that comprise each factor. The higher one's score, the more salient the issue is to the person.

RESULTS FOR BROTHERS

Six factors emerged in the data relating to brothers, including: Social Status/Role, Brotherly Deference to Priests, Priestly Role Clarity, Self-Determination: Role and Power, Tension with Priests, and Brotherhood Distinctiveness. Four demographic variables were useful in understanding the influence of these factors: Educational Degree, Type of Ministry, Age, and Type of Community. Each will be discussed in turn.

Educational Degree.   Three results of interest emerge concerning this variable. On Factor 1 (Social Status/Role), those with an associates degree had significantly higher concern for status than those with a Ph.D. On factor 2 (Brotherly Deference to Priests), those with graduate degrees were significantly less interested in seeing the role of brothers as one that provides essential services to the priest than those without an advanced degree. Finally, those with a Ph.D. were significantly less concerned with a more autonomous definition of brotherhood (factor 4) than those with a high school, A.A. or B.A. degree.

What emerges from these analyses is that a graduate, professional degree appears to provide a brother with a clearer definition of ministry and identity. Such educational training provides an individual greater autonomy as well as a measure of status. This sense of identity and purpose is clearly lacking in the 50% of brothers who do not have such a degree. These individuals see their role more closely attached to serving the priesthood. They also manifest a strong need for greater definition of their vocation.

Type of Ministry.   Two important results emerged for brothers as a function of the type of ministry they perform. Those involved in an educational ministry had a significantly lower score on factor 2 (Deference to Priests) than those in the remaining ministries, with the exception of those in 'administration'. Secondly, those in 'Education' are significantly less concerned with issues of self-determination and power (factor 4) than those in a parish ministry.

Being involved in an educational ministry may provide brothers with sufficient distance and distinctiveness from priests so that issues of autonomy and deference are not particularly relevant. This may be because a teaching brother finds himself in an environment that is controlled by brothers (i.e., a brother-supported school) and where priests play a more peripheral role. Further, such brothers may also have more education and, as noted earlier, have a clearer sense of vocation and higher status to begin with. In the parish setting the role of the brother is perceived to be secondary to the sacramental functions of the priest. Such brothers may find themselves overshadowed by the role of priests and thus are more likely to struggle with issues of vocational identity. This crisis may be exacerbated by the increasing role of laity in the Church as well as by the type of questions a theologically naive congregation may ask (e.g., ''How come you didn't become a priest?'' ''What is it that brothers do?'').

Age. In general, attitudes among brothers cluster according to two distinct age groups: (1) those 61 and above, and (2) those 18-60. The older group is significantly less concerned with issues of Status and Role (factor 1), and Autonomy and Power (factor 4). And they perceive less Tension with Priests (factor 5) than the younger group of brothers. The older group maintains greater Deference to Priests (factor 2) than does the younger group.

Two explanations can be generated to accommodate these findings. The first is that age has provided these older brothers with a greater sense of identity, or just less concern with the issues comprising this questionnaire. Secondly, it may be possible that the religious training these older brothers received provided a much clearer sense of brotherhood than today. Based on these results it is possible that deference to priests was more clearly emphasized previously than today. As the role of the brother, like that of the priest, continues to change to meet new demands, the traditional legacy of a brother's role as one of support to the priest may not only be obsolescent, but also a source of friction for younger members.

Type of Community. Brothers responding to the questionnaire live in one of two types of congregations: (1) the mixed community where brothers and priests live in common; and, (2) the community comprised of brothers only. Those in mixed communities were significantly more concerned with issues of Social Status (factor 1), Brotherly Deference (factor 2), and Self-Determination (factor 4) than those in a congregation whose members are only brothers. Those in a more homogeneous environment perceived significantly more Tension with Priests (factor 5) than those in a mixed community.

Brothers working in close proximity to priests evidence greater concern over issues of identity, status and autonomy. Under such circumstances brothers may find themselves in a secondary role to priests. In the parish setting, priests maintain an exclusive sacramental position. In mixed communities it is not uncommon for brothers to be prohibited from assuming positions of leadership and authority, even over other brothers. Thus, those in brothers-only communities may be seeking 'refuge' from such circumstances. That such individuals perceive greater tension with priests may also reflect a greater sensitivity to issues of priestly domination.

As was also mentioned earlier, although these kinds of situations may have been more consistent with a brother's vocation, the changing demands placed upon brothers as well as the possibility that a different type of person is seeking a religious calling, argue that the role of the brother needs reformulation from the perspectives of brothers of all ages. Close contact with priests appears to generate among certain groups of brothers a lack of clarity surrounding their vocational identity.

Summary. The major theme evolving from these data centers on the notion of identity. This is particularly true for those

brothers who live and/or work closely with priests. These individuals appear concerned about the apparent secondary role they
play with regard to priests. Possibly an increasing involvement of
the laity in the Church may complicate these feelings. However, as
these data indicate, those with advanced educational degrees,
living in a brothers-only community, or involved in a teaching
ministry appear to have a clearer sense of vocational clarity and
ministerial autonomy.

The next section will examine priests' responses and their
issues of interest. As will be seen, a different set of concerns
dominate their perceptions.

RESULTS FOR PRIESTS

The data related to priests indicated four factors of concern
(Table 4): Clericalism Awareness (factor 1), Functional and Sacramental Primacy of Priesthood (factor 2), Priesthood Complexity
versus Brotherhood Simplicity (factor 3), and Brotherhood
Fidelity (factor 4). Three demographic variables were found useful
in understanding the influence of these dimensions: Status (active
versus retired), Age, and Type of Community.

Status.   Retired priests see the role of the brother more
associated with service to priests (factor 2) than active priests.
Further, these retired respondents see brothers as remaining closer
to their original charisms than do younger priests (factor 4).
Finally, active priests perceive the priesthood as being more complex and facing more sophisticated issues than retired priests
(factor 3).

These analyses suggest that older priests maintain a more
traditional perception of brothers — that their position is one of
service to the priest, freeing him to pursue his sacramental role. As
such, a clear distinction is made between the two vocations and
older priests believe it should be maintained. Older priests may see

service to priests as being responsive to the original charisms of the brotherhood. These perceptions may be a source of tension for brothers in mixed communities.

Clearly, younger, active priests do not share this perspective. Although this group sees the role of the priest as evolving to meet increasingly complex social demands, there may also be a related perception that the role of brother is also in transition (however our data do not directly address this last issue). The next section will provide more detail of these analyses by examining different age groups separately.

Age. The age of priest respondents influenced results in 3 particular issues. Respondents between 41-50 years are significantly more sensitive to issues of clericalism and its impact on brothers than those 70+ years old (the retired category). Secondly, it appears that those 61 and above are significantly more committed to a belief in the primacy of the priesthood than those 18-60. Finally, those 70 and above see the priesthood as not being any more complex than it was when they were actively participating in their ministry.

These results clearly support and extend the findings of the previous section. Contemporary active priests see the role of the priest as being in transition. As it evolves to meet increasingly more complex social needs, there may be a growing recognition that priests can no longer single-handedly provide the required services. Although the older priests may prefer to maintain clear distinctions between the two vocations, younger priests appear to be more sensitive to these ''class'' distinctions. Particularly those 41-50 see these discriminations as having a negative impact on the brothers' roles by making their contributions appear less valuable and important.

Type of Community. Only one significant effect emerges between priests who live in a mixed community and those who live only with priests. Those in a mixed community perceive the role of the priest as becoming more sophisticated and complex than those in a priests-only residence.

It may be possible that mixed communities more strongly emphasize differences between the two vocations as well as maintaining brothers in a more service oriented role. Thus such priests may have a narrower view of the capabilities of a brother. Priests who live with other priests appear to treat brothers in a more collegial manner when they interact with them. Such priests may be exposed to brothers in different roles, such as teacher, administrator and therapist, rather than as cook, farm laborer, or housekeeper and thus react to brothers differently.

Summary.   Two particular issues appear to have dominated priests' responses to this questionnaire: the first concerns distinctions between the roles of priests and brothers; the second the negative impact such discrimination may have on the identity of the brother.

Older priests clearly see the brother as one who provides support to the ministry of the priest. His role is one of service and humility. These qualities are perceived as fundamental to the traditional role-identity of the brotherhood. For them, the priest maintains a role of primacy and exclusiveness not only in the Church but in the community as well. Although these older respondents maintain these stereotype perceptions, they see this division of labor as the cornerstone upon which the order is structured, while apparently respecting brothers for their work and seeming spiritual depth.

From the analyses of the brothers' responses, it was evident that issues of autonomy, identity and status dominated their responses. Certain segments of the brother population feel that their contributions are not only overshadowed by those of priests, but that the value of the contribution may also be minimized. The subsequent disenfranchisement which brothers experience may be reason enough to explain the tension perceived between brothers and priests.

These data indicated that those brothers who may be working/ serving older priests, and/or involved in the sacramental execution of a priest's duties, and/or with a limited education are those most likely to be expressing feelings of doubt and confusion over their vocational identity as well as experiencing some measure of tension in their interpersonal contacts within their community. Those who are in brothers-only communities, with advanced degrees, in an educational setting appear to have a clearer sense of vocational direction. Thus issues of clericalism and ministerial disenfranchisement among brothers appear limited to a particular subgroup of brothers.

Although only 5% of our brothers' sample fulfill all the above mentioned criteria, it should *not* be assumed that issues of clericalism, or brothers' needs for greater identity, status, and autonomy are restricted to a small "pocket" of individuals. Over 60% of brothers live in a mixed community, 46% do not have any advanced degree or professional training, and 35% are engaged in a ministry that may be designed to support the role of the priest (e.g., parish work, administration, administrative support, and manual labor). Clearly a large segment of the brothers' population finds itself in circumstances where the potential for experiencing clericalism and a sense of role confusion may be felt. A more accurate estimate of the extent to which clericalism has impacted the lives of brothers will be discussed in the next section.

However there are some clear signs of hope. Only a minority of priests, those in their 60's and 70's, maintain a view which subordinates the brother's role to the service of priests. The passage of time will certainly reduce their influence within communities. The majority of priests appears to reject these perceptions, and certain groups of priests are particularly sensitive to issues of clericalism (those in the 41-50 age range). That these are also those who are or will be assuming positions of leadership in their organizations suggests that positive institutional change may be in the offing. The sensitivity of younger priests to issues of clericalism should be reinforced. Finally, and perhaps most importantly, these relatively younger priests, although acknowledging that the role of priests is becoming more complex and is requiring more sophisticated skills on their part, do not see the priest as maintaining a supraordinate role to that of brothers. This suggests two possibilities.

First, it may indicate that there is a growing awareness among priests that a different role from brothers does not necessarily mean a "better" role. Just as the priest is called upon to perform certain functions, so too are brothers. Each fulfills roles serving specific purposes that allow the "whole" (i.e., the Church or Order) to continue to fulfill its mission. In other words, value labels are not being applied ostensibly to the increasing differentiation of the priestly and brotherly roles. A second interpretation may be that the perceived increasing social demands confronting priests necessitates that they draw on other sources to help facilitate their ministerial duties. The priest may not be able to deal adequately with the range of needs presented by any one person or group. Brothers may be a much needed resource that could augment the priest's interventions. In other areas, perhaps brothers should be allowed to assume responsibilities for many of the pastoral functions not specifically related to but traditionally performed by the priest. Over 53% of brothers occupy roles in the fields of education, health and social work. An expanded, well-defined approach to collaborative ministry needs further development. However, what remains apparent is the need to remove value labels and increase a spirit of cooperation and complementarity between priests and brothers. This would go far in addressing the basic issues raised by both groups.

This above section provided an overview of the more general issues that emerged in the data. The following section will directly examine responses to particular items included in the survey. Particular emphasis will be placed on the responses given by brothers.

ITEM ANALYSES

The last section of the questionnaire was devoted to brothers' perceptions and attitudes towards their vocation. Of particular interest was the question, "Have you ever felt oppressed, used, patronized, or in any way made to feel inferior by priests?" Over 66% of the brothers answered "yes." This two-thirds response rate was true regardless of whether the person was in a mixed or brothers-only community. Over 80% felt that their vocation could more fully be appreciated by priests and laity alike. Over 75% of those in a brothers-only community and over 55% of those in a mixed community felt that the presence of priests in an order restricted the degree to which brothers can assume positions of authority. Over 80% of brothers in both types of communities felt there is a need to revise the way authority is distributed in the order (i.e., brothers should be able to assume more leadership roles).

Despite such perceived limitations in the exercise of their vocations, over 90% of all brothers responded positively when asked, "If I had it to do again, I would become a brother." Although over 60% of all brothers see duties which support the role of the priest as fitting into their understanding of their vocation, over 85% of all brothers do not perceive the role of the brother to be less important than the role of the priest, and approximately 70% of all brothers (80% in brothers-only and 60% in mixed communities) do NOT want any change in the definition of what it means to be a brother.

What seems to emerge from these results is that brothers appear committed to their vocation and its inherent duties. At issue seems to be that brothers may not be getting the degree of validation of their services that they may feel they deserve. One way of making such an acknowledgment could take the form of accepting brothers into leadership/decision-making roles in the order.

When both priests and brothers were asked what single change would be the most influential in encouraging a more positive view of the brotherhood (both within religious and lay circles), 29.4% of the respondents (33% of the brothers and 26% of the priests) indicated that clearly identifying the brotherhood as a distinct religious vocation would do this. The second most frequent response (26% of the respondents; 21.5% brothers, 28% priests) was to develop a theology of brotherhood. There appears a distinct need to articulate more clearly the role and vocation of the brother. Such a step may have the effect of formalizing and validating the identity of brothers within the Church.

Impact of Ordination. This section asked brothers of mixed communities questions concerning the influence ordination has on their vocation. Respondents marked their responses to each statement on a 1 to 4, strongly disagree-strongly agree, scale.

Three items emerged with which these brothers particularly agreed: (1) Brothers should be allowed to assume the position of superior in the local community (average rating of 3.6 out of a possible 4); (2) The role of the brother should be equal in status to that of priests (average rating of 3.5); (3) It is the common commitment to religious life that both brothers and priests share that unites them (mean rating of 3.7). Three items emerged with which brothers particularly disagreed: (1)The presence of ordained priests unnecessarily distance them from others in their community (average rating of 1.7); (2)The presence of ordained priests in the community has unnecessarily influenced the direction of their vocation (mean rating of 1.7); (3)Issues surrounding ordination have put them in conflict with others in their community (mean rating of 1.9).

Thus among brothers the demand for greater access to leadership roles in the community recurs as a prominent theme. Ordination is NOT negatively perceived by brothers, it merely represents a different set of duties within the community. The roles of each vocation appear to complement one another. Priests and brothers share the same commitments and goals, though each performs specific tasks that contribute in their unique way to the overall success of their mission. Thus brothers argue that their role be valued. One means of recognizing the complementarity of functions as well as minimizing status differences and the effects of clericalism is to grant brothers their desired access to positions of leadership within their congregations.

Supporting this interpretation are the responses of both brothers and priests to the question, ''What ONE reason would be the MOST influential in persuading a brother to become a priest?'' Over 48% of the respondents (53.3%) of the brothers and 43.2% of the priests indicated, ''To be able to administer the sacraments.'' The next most frequent response (17.3% of the sample; 12% of the brothers and 22.7% of the priests) was ''Because priesthood provides the greatest range of ministerial options.''

Both brothers and priests share the perception that a brother would change his vocation in order to change the type of duties he would perform. Only 5% of the respondents (6.4% of the brothers and 3.7% of the priests) felt that such a change would be motivated by a need to achieve greater status in the Church. Thus especially for brothers, priesthood is not seen as either having a negative influence on their vocation or as a solution to their perceptions of being less valued.

The next two sections will examine all respondents' perceptions of the roles of both priests and brothers.

The Role of the Brother. Respondents were again presented with a series of statements to which they indicated their responses on a 1 to 4, strongly disagree-strongly agree, scale.

Both brothers and priests see the brotherhood as allowing one to make unique contributions of spiritual gifts to the Church (mean ratings of 3.6 and 3.5, respectively); and as a lifestyle that allows for a great freedom of career opportunities (mean ratings of 3.1 and 2.9, respectively). Both brothers and priests perceived the brotherhood as playing an important role in contemporary Church affairs (mean ratings of 3.2 and 2.8, respectively), and both disagree that this function is being compromised by the increasing role of laity in the Church (mean ratings of 2.1 and 2.2, respectively). Particularly brothers see their source of satisfaction as being derived from their selfless dedication to others (mean ratings of 3.4 for brothers and 3.0 for priests), and as such are happy to provide support work if it provides life to their community (3.2 for brothers and 3.0 for priests).

However both brothers and priests recognize that the issues of status and power between the two vocations detract from the brothers' ministry (mean ratings of 3.0 and 3.1, respectively). Both groups tend to agree that priests enjoy greater status and have more privileges than brothers (mean ratings of 2.9 and 2.8, respectively) and that ordination has led to a perception by brothers that their work is less significant than the sacramental work of priests (mean ratings of 2.8 and 2.7, respectively). Priests are slightly more in agreement with the statement, ''Brothers seem to feel inferior to priests'' than are brothers (mean ratings of 2.6 versus 2.3, respectively. This difference is statistically significant).

The Role of the Priest.   Respondents were again presented with a series of statements to which they indicated their responses on a 1 to 4, strongly disagree-strongly agree, scale.

Both brothers and priests agree that priests are: (1) asked to minister in a great variety of areas (mean ratings of 3.2 and 3.5, respectively);   (2) facing many more complex issues than just 10 years ago (mean ratings of 3.5 for both groups);   (3) more specialized since Vatican Council II, and require greater training (mean ratings of 3.2 for both groups);   (4) confronting more socially complex issues (mean ratings of 3.4 and 3.5, respectively). Both groups similarly disagree that the role of the priest has diminished since Vatican Council II (mean ratings of 2.2 for brothers and 2.1 for priests). Although the priesthood remains vibrant in its ministerial mission, both groups strongly disagree with the proposition that only priests should be called upon to provide leadership in the community (mean ratings of 1.3 for brothers and 1.4 for priests).

Summary. The above results clearly validate the roles of *both* brothers and priests. Both vocations are seen by all respondents as making critical contributions to the mission of the Church. Brothers find their vocational centering in their devotion to the service of others, generally in supportive roles to priests or distinctly separate from them, and in cooperating with the larger ecclesial mission of the Church. The priesthood confronts head-on the social and moral challenges produced by an increasingly complex and technical society. If the Church is to maintain an effective spiritual ministry, both priests and brothers recognize that previous perceptions of inferior roles of brothers need to be changed. Although priests may have (and continue to enjoy) greater status and ministerial freedom than brothers, all respondents recognize that this should not continue; brothers should also be called upon to provide leadership and direction within the community.

All respondents perceive a devaluation of the brothers' contribution to the community and the negative impact this has on brothers' morale. The attitudes evidenced in this questionnaire clearly acclaims the importance of the brotherhood, and the need to more fully involve and acknowledge brothers in more aspects of ministry. The final section of this report will attempt to synthesize the information provided in this entire survey through a series of conclusions.

Discussion

SEVERAL CONCLUSIONS may be drawn from this research. They are stated in the form of propositions and followed by a discussion.

I. Brothers Generally Believe that their Vocation to the Church is not fully Valued

The transition in the role of brothers since Vatican II has had both positive and negative consequences for the identity of brothers. As the role was differentiated from traditional interpretations and brothers assumed responsibilities not subordinated to the priesthood, the brotherhood entered a state of identity development. Many brothers achieved academic and professional success which may have increased their satisfaction with their identity as brothers. They were recognized for their professional contribution to the Church. But many other brothers felt tethered to traditional role definitions without any new and distinctive identity to enact. That which was experienced as development by some was experienced as diffusion by others.

Most brothers agree that their vocation in the Church is not clearly understood, nor is it fully valued. The challenge remains for brothers, in dialogue with other ministries in the Church, to define the particular theological and social dimensions of their life. Without a clear social and ecclesial identity, the role of the brother within the Church will likely remain diffuse and, therefore, undervalued by others.

II. The Brothers Who Feel that their Vocation is Not Fully Valued are those Who do not have an Advanced Degree (M.A. or Above), those Who Work in a Parish setting, and those Who Live in Mixed Communities.

The results suggest that the level of education, the ministry and the type of community to which a brother commits himself may each influence his perception of being valued. Brothers with less than a Masters Degree most often feel discounted as individual contributors to the mission of the Church or community.

Similarly, brothers who work within parish settings apparently feel less valued than those, for instance, who work in educational settings. The data support the perception that brothers who work with priests in parish settings often feel inferior to them. When the priest is identified as the primary leader of the community, the brother often feels subordinated both in role and esteem to the priest.

Finally, brothers who live in mixed communities perceive that they are less valued than those who live in exclusively brothers' communities. Again, the relationship between the priests and brothers of a mixed congregation apparently creates among brothers a sense of being subordinated to the priest. Brothers in all-brothers communities seemingly perceive that their vocation is more highly valued. Surely their access to positions of congregational leadership, their academic and professional status, and their relative independence from clerical control may influence their perceptions. That such brothers are higher in their perceived tension with priests may suggest that such individuals see such a community as a "refuge" from priests. They may seek it out in an attempt to find a clearer identity as a brother.

III. THE MAJORITY OF BROTHERS HAS BEEN MADE TO FEEL USED AND/OR OPPRESSED BY PRIESTS

The strength of these findings argues rather clearly that the relationship between brothers and priests has not been and still is not without significant difficulties. The CMSM task force appointed to study issues of inequality between priests and brothers suggested that attitudes of elitism and dominance among some priests continue to obstruct the realization of the Kingdom. Whether the word "clericalism" aptly describes this feeling of subordination among brothers to the authoritarian and hierarchical view, the perception that 66% of all brothers have experienced such oppression requires that congregations further understand the structures and role relationships which reinforce such perceptions.

IV. OLDER PRIESTS, PARTICULARLY THOSE WHO ARE RETIRED, MAINTAIN A PERCEPTION THAT THE BROTHER'S ROLE IS LESS IMPORTANT THAN THAT OF THE PRIEST

The specificity of the priestly role in the Church, its sacramental primacy and its status as a professional role, suggest to many priests that the proper role of the brother is somehow less important. Retired priests tend to hold this view significantly more than those who are active in the ministry. And those priests who are retired apparently see no discrepancy in the belief that status differentiates priests from brothers in an ecclesial community. Among older priests the proper identity of brothers and their status is viewed in relation to their perception of the esteem deserved by priests. Contrary to what may seem to be implied, these priests do not really think less of the integrity of brothers. They believe in the distinctive sacramental nature of priesthood in which the hierarchical role is pre-eminent among ecclesial ministries. They may distinguish the role of the brother as less important without necessarily implying any personal inferiority. Brothers on the other hand may not necessarily distinguish their role from their individual identity.

V. YOUNGER PRIESTS, PARTICULARLY THE COHORT BETWEEN 41-50 YEARS OF AGE, APPEAR SENSITIVE TO THE IMPACT OF CLERICALISM UPON BROTHERS

Priests between the ages of 41-50 years old exhibit significantly greater sensitivity to brothers and are aware of the impact of clericalism upon brothers. It is possible to conjecture that this group of priests had become attuned to issues of clericalism by virtue of their seminary education, by their involvement with lay ministers in pastoral settings, or by virtue of their exercise of community leadership. The data, however, does not support any conclusive explanations.

Many of the priests of this cohort would have been ordained as the changes of Vatican II began to be implemented. The role changes that occurred within the priesthood and religious congregations in general were often accompanied by dialogue and education. As newly ordained priests, the exact role previously enacted by priests was under review and some alteration. Brothers and priests began to mingle. Brothers assumed new roles and communities became more conscious of their shared values. Distinctions and forced separation were eliminated from many constitutions.

Among this cohort the movement toward lay ministry in the Church also allowed priests to be confronted with their own sense of elitism, even amidst brothers and lay associates of equal or superior competencies. The invitation to collaboration in ministry with other ministers perhaps allowed the priests of this age to realize that their presumed superiority was experienced as oppressive by brothers.

VI. BROTHERS APPEAR TO BE SEARCHING FOR GREATER VALIDATION OF THEIR ROLE. THE POSSIBLE SOLUTIONS THAT AROSE IN THE RESPONSES INCLUDED:

a. that since all religious work for the greater good of the Church, each contribution should be equally valued;

b. providing brothers with access to leadership roles in the community or order would distribute responsibility to members by virtue of their competence rather than by virtue of their role;

c. developing a firm theological and social role identity for brothers in the Church as well as encouraging vocations to the brotherhood would prove helpful.

VII. THE ROLE OF THE PRIEST IN THE CHURCH IS PERCEIVED
TO BE INCREASINGLY COMPLEX AND DEMANDING.

Brothers view themselves as essential partners in ministry with priests and they want to be recognized and valued for their distinctive service to the Church and their congregations. Over 50% of the brothers surveyed were involved in health, education, or social work. Performing their functions in these areas and witnessing to gospel values in diverse social contexts identifies in part the distinctive character of the brotherhood. As the Church recognizes increasingly that its mission involves social transformation as well as sacramental conversion, the roles of brothers and priests will be seen as distinctively complementary.

Ministry teams which incorporate all dimensions of social and ecclesial need should also emphasize the equality of services provided by all ministries. And within these teams leadership may be defined by virtue of the mission, the institution, or the expertise required to fill particular functions. The context of ministry and the particular needs of the people should generate leadership from within the community itself rather than assume leadership to be the domain of the priest alone.

VIII. This Survey Indicates that Attitudes which Differentiate Priests and Brothers in Terms of Status or Power have diminished.

The possibility for a new rapprochment between brothers and priests is strong. In order to reinforce attitudes which promote clarity, equality of service recognition, and the complementarity of roles between priests and brothers, continued dialogue is essential. As attitudes are reinforced with new visions, behaviors which have come to be identified as ''clerical'' may diminish, and a life of communion between brothers and priests may again be realized.

Table 1

Percentage of Brothers in Each of the Demographic Groupings

STATUS:
1) Brother 718
   (*actual number in*
   our sample)
2) Priest . . . . ——
3) Other . . . . ——

TYPE OF COMMUNITY:
1) Brothers only 37.0
2) Priests only . . . . . . ***
3) Mixed 63.0

ETHNIC ORIGIN:
1) Afro-American 7
2) Asian 1.3
3) Caucasian 91.4
4) Spanish-American 1.3
5) Hispanic-
   American 1.4
6) Other 3.9

HIGHEST EDUCATIONAL
DEGREE:
1) High School 23.9
2) Associates 5.0

3) Bachelors 16.9
4) Masters 43.3
5) Doctorate 8.0
6) Others 2.9

TOTAL NUMBER OF YEARS
IN FORMATION:
(*From end of navitiate*
to perpatual vows or final
commitment)
1) 0-1 . . . . 3.1
2) 2-5 . . . . 56.9
3) 6-10 . . . . 33.7
4) 11+ 6.3

AGE AT ENTERING ORDER
   18.5 (*median*)

ARE YOU CURRENTLY:
1) 90.4
2) Retired 9.6

YOUR MINISTREY:
1) Health 7.3

215

2) Education *42.7*
3) Parish Ministry *7.6*
4) Mission *2.5*
5) Administration *11.9*
6) Administrative
   support *5.7*
7) Social work *2.8*
8) Manual Labor *9.5*
9) Other *9.9*

AREA OF RESIDENCE:
1) Pacific (WA, OR,
   CA, HI, AK) *10.6*
2) Mountains (MT, ID,
   WY, NV, UT, CO,
   AZ, NM) *3.4*
3) West North Central
   (ND, SD, NE, KS,
   MN, IA, MO) ... *10.1*
4) East North Central
   (WI, MI, IL, IN,
   OH) *24.2*
5) West South Central (TX,
   OK, AR, LA),   *9.7*
6) East South Central (KY,
   TN, MS, AL) *4.2*
7) Middle Atlantic
   (NY, PA, NJ) ... *23.2*
8) New England (ME,
   VT, NH, MA, CT,
   RI *8.1*
9) South Atlantic (WV,
   VA, MD, DE, DC,

NC, SC, GA, FL) *6.6*

COMMUNITY DEMOGRAHPICS:
(*Approximately percentage of*)
1) Priest   32% (*median*)
2) Brothers   69% (*median*)
3) Average age of all
   members 53%
                  (*median*)

NUMBER OF YEARS
SINCE PERPETUAL VOWS:
1) 0 .... *4.8*
2) Up to 1 .... *1.4*
3) 2-4 .... *4.5*
4) 6-10 .... *7.0*
5) 11-15 .... *10.4*
6) 16-20 .... *10.0*
7) 21-25 .... *12.9*
8) 26-35 .... *24.6*
9) 36+ *24.3*

NUMBER OF YEARS
ORDAINED ***

YOUR AGE:
1) 18-30 .... *4.4*
2) 31-40 .... *18.0*
3) 41-50 .... *26.5*
4) 51-60 .... *21.2*
5) 61-70 .... *16.4*
6) 70+ *13.6*

Table 2

Percentage of Priests in Each of the Demographic Groupings

STATUS:
1) Brother   ___
2) Priest 675
   (*actual number in
   our sample*)
3) Other .... ___

TYPE OF COMMUNITY:
1) Brothers only ..... ***
2) Priests only 6.1
3) Mixed 93.9

ETHNIC ORIGIN:
1) Afro-American 1.0
2) Asian 0.4
3) Caucasian 91.2
4) Spanish-American 0.6
5) Hispanic-
   American 0.6
6) Other 6.1

HIGHEST EDUCATIONAL
DEGREE:
1) High School 0.9
2) Associates 0.6

3) Bachelors 15.5
4) Masters 59.2
5) Doctorate 21.3
6) Other 2.5

TOTAL NUMBER OF YEARS
IN FORMATION:
(*From end of novitiate
to perpetual vows or
final commitment*
1) 0-1 .... 1.5
2) 2-5 .... 44.1
3) 6-10 .... 28.5
4) 11+ 25.9

AGE AT ENTERING ORDER
  19.5 (*median*)

ARE YOU CURRENTLY:
1) Active 93
2) Retired 7

YOUR MINISTRY:
1) Health 4.6
2) Education 33.9

3) Parish ministry *33.2*
4) Mission work *3.6*
5) Administration *7.9*
6) Administrative
   support *1.9*
7) Social work *1.2*
8) Manual labor *0.1*
9) Other *13.5*

AREA OF RESIDENCE:
1) Pacific (WA, OR,
   CA, HI, AK) *14.1*
2) Mountains (MT, ID,
   WY, NV, UT, CO,
   AZ, NM) *4.8*
3) West North Central
   (ND, SD, NE, KS,
   MN, IA, MO) ... *10.9*
4) East North Central
   (WI, MI, IL, IN,
   OH) *21.0*
5) West South Central
   (TX, OK, AR, LA) *4.9*
6) East South Central
   (KY, TN, MS, AL) *2.1*
7) Middle Atlantic
   (NY, PA, NJ) ... *19.3*
8) New England (ME,
   VT, NH, MA, CT,
   RI) *11.3*
9) South Atlantic (WV,
   VA, MD, DE, DC,

   NC, SC, GA, FL) ...*11.6*

COMMUNITY DEMOGRAPHICS:
(*Approximately percentge of*)
1) Priest   *84.5% (median)*
2 Brothers   *15% (median)*
3) Average age of all
   members   *54% (median)*

NUMBER OF YEARS SINCE
PERPETUAL VOWS:
1) 0 .... *0.7*
2) Up to 1 .... *0.1*
3) 2-5 .... *4.3*
4) 6-10 .... *8.1*
5) 11-15 .... *7.9*
6) 16-20 .... *7.9*
7) 21-25 .... *12.1*
8) 26-35 .... *27.2*
9) 36+ *31.5*

NUMBER OF YEARS
ORDAINED   *24 (median)*

YOUR AGE:
1) 18-30 .... *2.2*
2) 31-40 .... *16.7*
3) 41-50 .... *23.7*
4) 51-60 .... *25.0*
5) 61-70 .... *20.0*
6) 70+ *12.3*

Table 3

**Factor Dimensions Derived from the Responses
Given by Brothers**

Results for Brothers

FACTOR 1:   *Social Status/Role*

ITEMS INCLUDE:

- — Makes the public less aware of the charisms of the brotherhood
- — Makes priests more highly valued in both Church and lay activities
- — Ordination has led to a perception of brothers that their work is less significant than the sacramental work of priests
- — The role of the brother has been diminished by the action of priests

FACTOR 2:   *Brotherly Deference to Priests*

ITEMS INCLUDE:

- — Priests should be given the highest respect
- — The presence of ordained priests more clearly defines my obligations to the community

— The role of brother is to provide essential services to the priest so
he may be free to pursue his ministerial duties
— Humility and patience are the characteristics of a true brother
— Brothers should be happy to provide support (e.g., administra-
tive/logistical/manual) to priests in their ministry

FACTOR 3:   *Priestly Role Clarity*

ITEMS INCLUDE:

— To achieve a better sense of ministerial identity
— To achieve greater status in the Church
— To be able to administer the sacraments
— To feel better about the type of service he can provide

FACTOR 4:   *Self-Determination, Role and Power*

ITEMS INCLUDE:

— Developing a theology of brotherhood
— Promoting a more self-determining view of brotherhood
— Letting brothers define their own vocation in the Church
— Brothers should be allowed to assume the position of superior in
the local community

FACTOR 5:   *Tension with Priests*

ITEMS INCLUDE:

— There is a tension in our community concerning the role of
priests
— Ordination creates an unnecessary social distinction in the
community

Table 3 221

— The presence of ordained priests unnecessarily distances me from others in my community
— The presence of ordained priests in my community has unnecessarily influenced the direction of my vocation

FACTOR 6: *Brotherhood Distinctiveness*

ITEMS INCLUDE:

— Encouraging brothers of mixed communities to develop a lifestyle apart from that of priests
— Brothers are more faithful to the original charisms of their founders than priests
— Brothers involved in active ministry seem to be more contemplative than priests
— Prohibiting brothers from becoming priests

Table 4

Factor Dimensions Derived from the Responses Given by Priests

---

Results for Priests

FACTOR 1: *Clericalism Awareness*

ITEMS INCLUDE:

- Ordination has promoted a sense of elitism among priests
- Ordination has led to a perception of brothers that their work is less significant than the sacramental work of the priest
- Ordination has left brothers without a clear sense of identity
- Ordination has entitled priests to education, travel and other benefits not given to brothers

FACTOR 2: *Functional and Sacramental Primacy of Priesthood*

ITEMS INCLUDE:

- The role of the brother is to provide essential services to the priest so he may be free to pursue his ministerial duties
- Ordination has provided a useful distinction that must not be blurred

— Ordination does serve to elevate a person to a higher stature by virtue of its sacramental power
— Some distinctions between brothers and priests need to be maintained

FACTOR 3: *Priesthood Compexity versus Brotherhood Simplicity*

ITEMS INCLUDE:

— There are increasing demands being placed on the priesthood to confront more socially complex issues
— Contemporary priests face many more complex issues than just 10 years ago
— The priesthood has become more differentiated because of increasing social needs
— The role of the priest has become more specialized since Vatican Council II, requiring greater training on his part

FACTOR 4: *Brotherhood Fidelity*

ITEMS INCLUDE:

— Brothers are more faithful to the original charisms of their founders than priests
— Brothers involved in active ministry seem to be more contemplative than priests
— Religious priests have wandered too far from the original charisms of their founders

Biographical Sketches

REV. STEPHEN TUTAS, S.M.

In his second term as president of the Conference of Major Superiors of Men, he is a former superior general of his congregation, the Marianists.

REV. ROLAND FALEY, T.O.R.

Former superior general of the Third Order Regular Franciscans, he is now Executive Director of the Conference of Major Superiors of Men in Silver Spring, Maryland. He has written several times for publication in the past.

REV. JAMES FITZ, S.M.

A member of the Society of Mary (Marianists). Presently he is a member of the provincial council and administration for the Cincinnati Province. He is the Assistant for Religious Life, having as his focus: formation, spiritual development, community development and collaboration with the laity. He served as Director of Novices from 1979-1985. Prior to that he was Coordinator for Adult Religious Education for the Diocese of Kalamazoo, Michigan. Previous publications include articles on religious life and spirituality in *Review for Religious* and *Human Development*.

REV. ROBERT SCHREITER, C.PP.S.

A Priest of the Society of the Precious Blood and professor of theology at the Catholic Theological Union in Chicago. He writes on questions of theology and culture and is the author of *Constructing Local Theologies* (Orbis Books, 1985). He also serves as Vice Provincial of the Cincinnati Province of his religious institute and as the formation director for its students in theology.

REV. THOMAS E. CLARKE, S.J.

A theologian and writer, he lives in New York City. He taught systematic theology at Woodstock College for twenty years; he was on the staff of Gonzaga Renewal Center, Monroe, New York for four years, and was a research fellow at the Woodstock Center in Washington, D.C., for four years. His most recent publication is *Playing in the Gospel: Spiritual and Pastoral Models* (Sheed and Ward, 1986), and Sheed and Ward will also publish his study guide, *Christian Living in the U.S. Culture*. He also contributed to the CMSM volume edited by David Fleming, S.M., *Religious Life at the Crossroads* (Paulist, 1985).

BR. MARTIN HELLDORFER, F.S.C.

A Christian Brother with a doctorate in ministry. he is a licensed psychotherapist presently on the staff at St. John Vianney Hospital in Downington, Pennsylvania. Previous to this employment he was a therapist and administrator at the House of Affirmation. He holds degrees in theology (La Salle University), chemistry (Notre Dame University), and a doctor of ministry degree (pastoral counseling) from Andover Newton. His writings include numerous articles in journals and periodicals as well as two books: *The Work Trap* and *Prayer, A Guide When Troubled*.

REV. JUSTIN DER, O.F.M., Cap.

Before his untimely death in Febuary, 1987, Fr. Der was chancellor of the Diocese of Pittsburgh. He held degrees in canon law, education and philosophy and had been during his career a teacher, counselor, parochial minister and military chaplain. He was named a judge in the tribunal of the Diocese of Pittsburgh in 1978, and was a Consultor to the Holy Office.

SR. MARGARET CARNEY, O.S.F. and *SR. SHEILA CARNEY, R.S.M.*

Sr. Margaret is currently a doctoral candidate in Franciscan spirituality in Rome. She has been assistant Vicar for Religious in the Diocese of Pittsburgh and a member of her order's general council. She has taught Franciscan spirituality in the Philippines and at St. Bonaventure University in New York. Her sister, Sr. Sheila, is a Pittsburgh Sister of Mercy. In twenty years of religious life her ministry has been primarily focused in education and spiritual formation. She has taught in elementary and secondary schools as well as St. Vincent College and Seminary in Latrobe, Pennsylvania. She has been director of formation for her congregation and has done spiritual direction and retreat work. She is currently superior general of her congregation.

MR. PETER GILMOUR

A faculty member of the Institute of Pastoral Studies, Loyola University, Chicago. Previous to teaching at Loyola, he taught at St. George High School, Evanston, Illinois, and was chairperson of the religion department there. He also taught at St. Patrick High School, Chicago, where he co-founded and directed *I-Project*, an interdisciplinary studies mini-school for 160 sophomore students. He is author of *The Emerging Pastor* (Sheed and Ward 1986), a book about non-ordained Catholic pastors in the United States; *Praying Together* (St. Mary's Press, 1978), a book of group prayer experiences for high school students, and several teacher guides and manuals. He received a doctorate from the University of St. Mary of the Lake, Mundelein, Illinois, in 1985. He lives in Rogers Park near Chicago.

BR. PATRICK HANSON, C.P.

A member of the Congregation of the Passion for nearly twenty years. He has been a high school teacher and administrator and vocation director for his community and for the Archdiocese of Chicago. He is currently co-director of the Office for Religious in the Archdiocese of Chicago. He served on the board of the National Assembly of Religious Brothers and was its president from 1983-1985, and he was one of the twelve brothers who wrote the "Washington Statement on the Call to Brotherhood."

BR. MICHAEL McGINNISS, F.S.C.

An associate professor of religion at La Salle University in Philadelphia, he has been a Christian Brother since 1965. He has taught in Christian Brothers' high schools in Philadelphia and Pittsburgh and on the faculty of Washington Theological Union in Silver Spring, Maryland. He received an M.A. and Ph.D. in theology from the University of Notre Dame. He is a frequent consultant to parishes on questions of renewal and the development of new ministries. He lectures and writes on theological reflection in ministerial education and on the relationship of ecclesiology and the religious life. Presently he is editor of the yearly publications of the Christian Brothers' North American Spirituality Seminar, the most recent being *Risky Business: Brotherhood in American Culture*.

DAVID J. NYGREN, C.M.

Received his Ph.D. in Psychology from Boston University. He is a researcher, teacher and an active consultant on issues of leadership, management and governance in theological schools, hospitals, and other non-profit organizations. He is presently Adjunct Assistant Professor of Psychology at Boston University and Research Associate in the Center for Applied Social Science at Boston University.

RALPH L. PIEDMONT

Received his B.A. degree (1980) in psychology and history, summa cum laude, from Iona College and his M.A. degree (1984) in psychology from Boston University, where he is currently completing his Ph.D. in personality psychology. Aside from being a part-time Instructor at the University of Massachusetts-Boston, he is also an independent research consultant specializing in survey sampling, questionnaire development and statistical analyses. He has two major areas of research interest. The first concerns achievement motivation, particularly in women, and the variables which facilitate and inhibit its expression. The second centers on psychological assessment — deriving more accurate, empirically based procedures for predicting behavior. He has published several articles in these areas, including most recently, "An interactional difference in achievement orientation using two different achievement scales". He is also a member of Psi Chi, Phi Alpha Theta, and Delta Epsilon Sigma as well as a member of the American Psychological Association.

ABBOT JEROME THEISEN, O.S.B.

Abbot of St. John's Abbey, Collegeville, Minnesota, since 1979. He was professed as a monk of that abbey in 1952 and ordained in 1957. He received his S.T.D. from St. Anselm's College in Rome in 1966, serving meanwhile as a professor of theology at St. John's University beginning in 1960. He was novice master of St. John's Abbey from 1975-1978.

REV. JORDAN HITE, T.O.R.

A civil and canon lawyer, a writer and editor, he is also a teacher and spiritual director at Mt. Assisi Monastery in Loretto, Pennsylvania, where he also exercises the office of Vicar Provincial for his province.

BR. PHILIP ARMSTRONG, C.S.C.

Currently assistant general of the Congregation of Holy Cross in Rome, he has previously been provincial of the Midwest Province in the United States and taught and administered in secondary schools in Ghana, West Africa, including a term as rector of the archdiocesan minor seminary. He has also served as teacher, administrator and counselor in high schools and in a boys' home in the United States.